NEW HORIZONS IN CRIMINOLOGY

IMAGINATIVE CRIMINOLOGY
Of Spaces Past, Present and Future

Lizzie Seal and Maggie O'Neill

BRISTOL
UNIVERSITY
PRESS

This paperback edition first published in Great Britain in 2021 by

Bristol University Press
University of Bristol
1-9 Old Park Hill
Bristol
BS2 8BB
UK
t: +44 (0)117 954 5940
e: bup-info@bristol.ac.uk

Details of international sales and distribution partners are available at
bristoluniversitypress.co.uk

© Bristol University Press 2021

British Library Cataloguing in Publication Data
A catalogue record for this book is available from the British Library

978-1-5292-0268-7 hardcover
978-1-5292-0273-1 paperback
978-1-5292-0272-4 ePub
978-1-5292-0270-0 Mobi
978-1-5292-0265-6 ePdf

Cover design by Bristol University Press
Front cover image: Maggie and Clare taken on a Leverhulme Walk led by Clare Qualmann.
The bridge is a site from Clare's night walks with walkwalkwalk.

Contents

List of figures and tables

Figures

Tables

NEW HORIZONS IN CRIMINOLOGY

Series editor: Professor Andrew Millie, Department of Law and Criminology, Edge Hill University, UK

Preface

Books in the New Horizons in Criminology series are by leading authors and reflect cutting-edge thought and theoretical developments in criminology. As an editor I want to attract authors who are doing work that is exciting and creating genuinely new horizons for criminology. Lizzie Seal and Maggie O'Neill are two authors that I admire, and I have been keen for them to be involved in the series in some way. That they chose to write this book together is a bonus! Maggie is known for important work with asylum seekers and sex workers, especially that which employs participatory and arts-based research methods – in particular, ethno-mimesis and walking methods (e.g. O'Neill and Hubbard, 2010). Lizzie's work is equally groundbreaking, especially her historical work on women who kill (2010) and capital punishment (2015). Seal and O'Neill have worked together before, and in their previous collaboration (O'Neill and Seal, 2012) they drew on cultural criminology to explore portrayals of transgression, subversion of these portrayals and the possibility of resistance. In this new book they take this further by suggesting an imaginative criminology that also considers the spatiality of transgression. Their focus is on 'spaces and places of transgression as lived, portrayed and imagined'.

For Seal and O'Neill, the book's aim is 'to argue for and do imaginative criminology'. Drawing inspiration from Mills' (1959) 'sociological imagination', the authors see imaginative criminology as bringing attention to social structure, place in history, the biographical and experiential. Seal and O'Neill use an array of imaginative methodologies to make this possible. Examples are from real life and fiction, including spaces of confinement, liminal spaces of borders and dystopian spaces of fiction. Oral histories are seen alongside cultural representations to explore how specific spaces and places are 'remembered as sites of transgression, exclusion, resistance and possibility'. One example is Australia's 'stolen generations', the removal of Indigenous children from their families between 1910 and 1970. The authors consider how this is remembered and culturally represented – for instance, through the book *Follow the Rabbit Proof Fence* and the film *Rabbit Proof Fence*. The authors also look at the Magdalene Laundries in Ireland, which housed poor and 'deviant' young women, including how they have been portrayed in documentary and in films such as '*Philomena*'. Seal and O'Neill then consider writing projects in prison, the importance of memories and relationships in prisoners' writing, and the portrayal of spaces of confinement – how 'inside' compares to 'outside'. The authors draw on arts-based methodologies – including film and walking ethnographies – to look at spaces of migration. The focus is on border spaces and camps, illustrated by work with asylum seekers and migrants in camps in Greece, France, Jordan and Melilla in North Africa. Attention shifts to imagined spaces of violence and transgression, particularly in Canada and Northern Ireland. In Canada the authors draw on the experience of a 'missing and dead women's Memorial March' in Downtown Vancouver. The aim of the march is to bring attention to women who are missing or have been murdered, 'who are Indigenous, poor, including women who sell sex, use drugs and are homeless or living in hostels and shelters'. In Northern Ireland the authors use arts-based participatory methods with citizens to consider various architectures of conflict. Seal and O'Neill then move to dystopian and speculative fiction such as *The Hunger Games* and *Red Rising*. They argue for greater criminological attention on fiction and how it influences 'cultural imaginings of social control, repression and resistance'.

Over recent decades the subject of criminology has been through several 'turns' – including a cultural turn, a visual turn and a spatial turn. This book is inspired by all three but takes the reader in an imaginative direction. Seal and O'Neill should be congratulated for producing this challenging and illuminating little book. They make a convincing argument for greater emphases on spatial, relational, reflective and discursive understandings of social justice – what they see as transformational justice. Criminology needs authors like Lizzie Seal and Maggie O'Neill and this book is highly recommended.

References

Mills, CW (1959) *The Sociological Imagination*, Oxford: Oxford University Press.

O'Neill, M and Hubbard, P (2010) 'Walking, Sensing, Belonging: Ethno-mimesis as Performative Praxis', *Visual Studies*, 25(1): 46–58.

O'Neill, M. and Seal, L. (2012) *Transgressive Imaginations: Crime, Deviance and Culture*, Basingstoke: Palgrave Macmillan.

Seal, L. (2010) *Women, Murder and Femininity: Gender Representations of Women Who Kill*, Basingstoke: Palgrave Macmillan.

Seal, L. (2015) *Capital Punishment in Twentieth-Century Britain: Audience, Justice, Memory*, Abingdon: Routledge.

Imaginative Criminologies of Space: the Spaces of Imaginative Criminology

Imaginative criminology explores the spaces and places of transgression as lived, portrayed and imagined. These include spaces of control or confinement (homes for Indigenous children, Magdalene laundries, prisons and refugee camps), borders that constitute marginalised and liminal places and spaces that are betwixt and between (peace walls and border lines), as well as fictional dystopias. It pays attention to how these spaces are experienced, understood, imagined and remembered as sites of transgression, exclusion, resistance and possibility. In our previous book, we examined historical and contemporary 'transgressive imaginations' and resistances in relation to the 'outsider' the 'criminal' and the 'deviant' through the genres of art, film, literature and ethnographic research (O'Neill and Seal, 2012). Here, we extend our analysis to grapple with the significance of transgression as it is imagined and lived in space.

Imaginative 'criminologies' is perhaps more apposite than imaginative criminology. The term is not intended to connote a particular perspective (indeed, this would undermine imagination) or a new type of criminology. Rather, it refers to work with certain characteristics. One of these is an 'increasing focus on cultural artefacts and institutions' (Frauley, 2015a: 618) and what Jacobsen (2014) refers to as the poetic dimensions of criminology. Imaginative criminologists borrow 'insights from artistic or literary sources' (p 2) and from their associated academic disciplines (O'Neill and Seal, 2012). Such work is flourishing and here we intend to make a further contribution to its expansion.

While criminology is frequently understood as the study of crime and criminal justice, and its methods as those of conventional social science, such as surveys and interviews, it is not contained or constrained by these definitions. For example, Young (2011: 13) in *The Criminological Imagination* critiques mainstream criminology's lack of imagination, evidenced by an almost singular focus on positivism, 'quasi-scientific rhetoric' and administrative criminology that works in favour of or legitimates neoliberal politics and offers cultural criminology as an antidote. This is a cultural criminology constituted through ethnographic work and phenomenological approaches.

Carlen (2010) in her book *A Criminological Imagination*, a selection of her work (over 30 years), delivers a deconstructionist, reflexive and critical analysis on punishment, prison and penal reform that invites readers to imagine a better world, serving the interests of justice and where 'the ordering of things can always be otherwise'. She offers 'three working beliefs' that underpin her 'practice of imaginative criminology'. First, an ontological belief about the social world: that everything that is could be different. Second, a belief about the task of social science: that it is more important to account for social phenomena than it is to count them. And third, a belief about the task of (academic) criminology: that one rationale for investigating the means of contemporary law breaking, and the social responses to it, is to imagine the 'conditions for them being otherwise' (Carlen, 2010: 1; cf Carlen, 2017: 20). The concept of criminal justice must remain imaginary (that is, impossible to realise) in societies based on unequal and exploitative relations. In summary, Carlen states that the project of the criminological imagination is to 'demonstrate that contemporary penal justice is both just and unjust, both possible and impossible, and with conditions of existence that have infinite possibilities for change' (2010: xiii).

Although common sense tells us that criminology must be primarily concerned with crime, Frauley (2015a) persuasively argues that criminology is more about ordering than it is about crime. At a stroke, this expands criminology's purview considerably. For Frauley (p 625), there is no need for the criminal justice system to be the 'source of orienting precepts' for criminologists. Imaginative criminology should, of course, pay attention to crime and the criminal justice system; it should simply not be confined to these as possible areas for analysis and research. The sociology of deviance, an important strand of criminology's DNA, established a strong tradition of the critical analysis of ordering and its transgression and it is to this lineage that imaginative criminology belongs (see Erikson, 1962; Becker, 1963; Cohen, 1971). Taking transgression as the central focus makes ordering a suitable orienting precept for this book as the transgressive is that which disturbs or contravenes established order.

Our methodological approach is avowedly cultural in its use of critical and cultural theory and creative methodologies and extends our prior use of filmic and archival research, visual and sensory ethnography, and biographical and participatory arts research to include walking and mobile methods as well as fictive research and analysis. This attention to creativity and representation extends and deepens the criminological imagination as urged by Young (2011) and Carlen (2010). What constitutes an imaginative criminological methodology for us is attention to the micrology of lived experience, the forms and ways of telling, to undertake what Back and Puwar (2012) call 'live methods' that open up the potential for how we 'do' criminology imaginatively. Central to our project is the importance of engaging with the philosophical, ethical and psycho-social aspects of transgression, confinement and ordering.

Our focus here is on the imaginative spaces of criminology in art, fictive texts, and archival and ethnographic research, as well what Young (1996: 16) defines as the 'imagined': the 'written and the pictorial: the linguistic turns and tricks, the framing and editing devices in and through which crime becomes a topic, obtains and retains a place in discourse'. We pay attention to the representations of transgression and ordering: the fictional, mediatised representations and imaginaries in fictive texts, creative writing, television drama and films, as well as in the buildings, spaces and places of crime and transgression – the spaces of imaginative criminology.

In *Transgressive Imaginations* (O'Neill and Seal, 2012) we argued that criminologists must acknowledge that 'everyday life is lived in the imaginary' (Young, 2008: 27) and the reactions of a viewer or reader to representations of crime, deviance and transgression are part of their everyday lived experience of these phenomena. As readers and viewers we 'draw on and add to the repertoire of images, ideas and meanings that are available to us about crime' (Clarke, 2001: 73). This is part of the landscape of imaginative criminology that we outline in this chapter. We also extend our case for the importance of cultural criminology in developing a radical democratic imaginary, in enabling us to think otherwise, and in facilitating public scholarship on these cultural issues. First it is helpful to examine the *forms* of imaginative criminology[ies] before moving on to discuss the politics and spaces of imaginative criminology.

The forms of imaginative criminology

Fiction, be it in the form of novels, short stories, TV programmes, films or plays, offers great potential for criminologists. The portrayal of 'complex and layered social realities that can be explored criminologically and sociologically' can help us to analyse ordering and transgression (Frauley, 2010: 13). What Frauley describes as 'fictional realities' enable engagement with the cultural realm and examination of the 'symbolic dimension of social reality' (p 34). He identifies three ways in which criminology has employed fiction. The first is cultural criminology's attention to the symbolism and meanings constructed in fictional sources. The second is Rafter's (2006; 2007) exploration of films as sources of cultural information about crime, and the third is Ruggiero's (2003) approach to novels as sources which illuminate, and help us to work through, real life issues. All three of these criminological engagements with fiction are drawn on in this book.

The poetic dimensions of criminology are also concerned with visual representations. Images of crime, harm, transgression and punishment proliferate in contemporary life and constitute an important means through which cultural meanings are built – they are arguably as, if not more, important to conveying 'the "story" of crime and crime control' as words (Hayward, 2010: 4). A diversity of ways exists for imaginative criminologists to comprehend the visual but, crucially, doing so opens up new possibilities and directions for criminological analysis (Carrabine, 2012; 2018), as well as ethical questions about the consumption of images of pain and suffering (Carrabine, 2012; Walklate et al 2016).

Gaining insights from fictional and artistic sources and storytelling is an important strand of imaginative criminology as we explore throughout this book. For example, detective fiction provides alternative ways of seeing and experiencing/exploring crime and can enable us to reflect on how we think about, imagine and understand relationships between what is right and wrong, social order and disorder, and the relational dimensions of crime and crime control (Clarke, 2001). Fiction opens up new questions and potentially offers 'alternative approaches to investigating the social world', which complement criminology (Page and Goodman, 2018: 3). Narrative criminology is another figuration that puts stories from interviews and ethnographic fieldwork at the centre of criminological analysis (Prosser and Sandberg, 2015 Fleetwood, 2014). There is, of course, a long history of conducting life story interviews and biographical research in criminology. Carlen's (1985) *Criminal Women* is a classic example and, in the four life stories presented in the book, the relationship between biography and history is writ large. More recently McGarry and Keating (2010) take up the argument that biographical research is valuable for contemporary criminological theory and especially for victimology.

For Wright Mills (1959 [1970]) this relationship between biography and history is part of the promise and challenge of the *sociological imagination*, which connects individual experience of 'private troubles' with broader social structures and processes. 'The sociological imagination enables us to grasp history and biography and the relations between the two within society. That is its task and its promise' (Wright Mills, 1970: 6). He figures imagination as the capacity to shift from one perspective to another – from the impersonal and remote to the intimate. Indeed, we have previously argued that methodologies that 'incorporate the voices of citizens through biographical and participatory methodologies can enlighten and raise awareness but also crucially create and sustain spaces for democratic discourse, uncover hidden histories and produce critical reflexive texts that may help to mobilise social change' (O'Neill and Seal, 2012: 8). Examining how transgression and ordering are constructed, made, understood, experienced and challenged needs historical analysis, biographical, ethnographic and participatory research, as well as analysis of media and fictive cultural forms and practices.

Another way of doing creative and imaginative criminological research is to extend this further to employ creative approaches based on art and literature or that involve collaborating with artists. O'Neill calls this 'ethno-mimesis' (O'Neill et al, 2001; O'Neill, 2004, 2017) – the combination or intersection of ethnographic, biographical and participatory research *with* art forms that may involve conducting research using arts-based methods, theatre, performance, walking and/or representing research in art forms. She argues that 'finding alternative, creative ways of re-presenting ethnographic research is part of the duty we have as interpreters and producers of knowledge' (2004: 219). Working with performance artists to represent the life stories of sex workers and with visual artists to facilitate the life stories of Bosnian refugees within the context of participatory research (the 'subjects' of research are the 'co-producers' of the research) and participatory arts enables phenomenological and reflexive research to be produced. This research is 'multi-vocal' and gives rise to 'sensuous knowing' that tells stories that might be impossible to tell in words alone, that might be 'unsayable' (O'Neill, 2004; 2017). Collaborating with artists to produce research data in art forms such as music, theatre, creative writing and participatory arts enables us to access a richer understanding of the complexities of lived experience that may throw light on broader social processes, structures and practices; and reach a wider population, beyond academia.

Such creative methodologies form the basis for much of the discussion in this book. In our approach to both critically analysing and doing imaginative criminology we follow Wright Mills in underscoring 'the cultural meaning of the social sciences' (1970: 8).

Chapter 4 draws on historical, narrative and ethnographic/mobile criminological research from two different prison-based creative writing projects. Chapters 5 and 6, on border spaces and urban spaces of violence and transgression, explore findings from ethno-mimetic (O'Neill, 2001) arts-based methods such as film, photography and walking ethnographies.

The politics of imaginative criminology

Imaginative criminology, like all criminology, involves doing politics (Frauley, 2015a). As Walklate and Jacobsen (2017: 6) argue, 'questions of imaginative epistemologies become intertwined with those of geography and democracy'. Related to issues of reinvigorating criminology with creative approaches, or borrowing insights from creative sources, is the larger issue of the criminological imagination. How criminologists conceive of their research questions, methodologies, writing and allegiances is vital to consider. Young (2011) is among several criminologists who have returned to Wright Mills's (1959) classic text on the sociological imagination in order to highlight its relevance for contemporary criminology (see also Barton et al, 2007; Frauley, 2015b). He asserts that the imagination is tied to transformative politics; it will challenge the acceptance of the way things are. For Carlen (2017: 19), imaginative criminology 'is well-designed to be a bridge between critical criminology and a critical politics of criminal justice policy'. Returning to the contention that criminology is more about ordering than it is about crime, we could include within this a critical politics of different forms of confinement and control that goes beyond criminal justice.

What kind of criminology is necessary in order to develop such critiques? Young (2011) takes aim at 'nomothetic' research, which develops general laws and arguments about social phenomena, intended to have global and timeless application. The denial of specificity is linked to the projection of western (and, frequently, American) values of individualism in social science research findings and their associated policy recommendations (Walklate and Jacobsen, 2017). Imaginative criminology must offer critical resistance to the colonial heritage 'that taints much contemporary criminological work' (p 6). It must also recognise that knowledge is not neutral but rather is interrelated with culture and the exercise of power (p 6). The alternative to nomothetic research is that which recognises historical particularity, employing case studies and other forms of in-depth (or 'idiographic') enquiry (Frauley, 2015a). This does not mean that there is no possibility for more widely applicable arguments, but that in these the local becomes linked to the global, and the personal becomes linked to the collective (Young, 2011).

Jacobsen (2014) proposes that imaginative criminology rests on the tripod of cultural, critical and creative criminology. We made a similar proposal, termed 'cultural/critical' criminology, in our previous book, *Transgressive Imaginations* (2012). We argued for the vitality of 'the art of thinking critically and creatively for developing and sustaining a criminological imagination' (p 158) and emphasised the need for innovative methodologies and attention to cultural representations in order to deal in complexity, challenge dominant images and stereotypes, and reflect the resistance and liveable lives of those who are marginalised. We now explicate our two underpinning concepts for doing imaginative criminology: the imaginary and transgression. In doing so, we also make clear the politics of our approach as rooted in radical democratic pluralism (Laclau and Mouffe, 1985; O'Neill and Seal, 2012).

The imaginary

The social imaginary refers to a society's imaginings and to its group ethos. It comprises the personal imagination of individuals and cultural representations, and is institutionalised, for example in court decisions or in the nature of prison regimes (Strauss, 2006; on its institutionalisation in relation to penality see Carlen, 2008). Tucker (2005: 43) draws on Castoriadis to highlight the 'importance of images and fantasy understanding collective action and public life'. The creative imagination, not rationality, is universal to human societies. The social imaginary creates a universe of meaning for individuals and 'brings forth modes of being' (Tucker, 2005: 52).

The shared social imaginary provides the basis for imagining the membership of the collective and its boundaries – for example, through imagining the nation (see Anderson, 1983). However, while members of the collective might recognise and understand a shared ethos, they do not all imagine its membership, or interpret politics and culture, in the same way. This is mediated by social positioning along axes of class, gender, race and so forth. Against a dominant social imaginary, there is a plurality of other group imaginaries (Laclau and Mouffe, 1985; Yuval-Davis and Stoetzler, 2002). The imaginary of individuals is shaped by both the wider collective and their own position within it, but also has an integrity of its own (Cornell, 1998; Strauss 2006).

Images and fantasy play a role in this plurality, which we argue underlines the importance of the imaginary to criminology. As Yuval-Davis and Stoetzler (2002) argue, images and imaginings need to be taken as seriously as knowledge. The imagination can transgress established patterns of thinking and acting, and can re-envisage existing power relations. Struggles over meaning and belief inspire creativity, which in turn provides the images of new ways of life (Tucker, 2005). Fantasy and images are essential to envisioning – and creating – the good society (Castoriadis, 1987). For individuals, the imaginary domain is a sanctuary that should be protected (Cornell, 1998). Cornell (p 28) conceptualises this as a 'moral and psychic space in which to orient ourselves', offering the chance to become a unique person. Freedom of personality requires the imaginary domain. In addition to collective visions of the good society, individuals should be able to preserve a valued sense of self and engage in dignified self-representation.

We understand the imaginary as having three different but interconnected elements. The social imaginary refers to the wider collective and can be understood as consonant with the imagined community of the nation (Anderson, 1983) but also potentially the relational, discursive and reflective principles of social justice (Hudson, 2006). The social imaginary is not unified or monolithic, but contains different group imaginaries along the lines of region, race, gender and sexuality. Group imaginaries may be alternatives, or counter, to dominant social imaginaries. The individual imaginary is shaped by the social and group imaginaries but is not reducible to these. Cornell's (1998) concept of the imaginary domain highlights the importance of the individual imaginary as offering sanctuary and freedom, as well as a means to imagine belonging and one's relation to others.

Political struggle – and political change – 'depend[s] in part on the ability to imagine alternative worlds' (Smith, 1998: 9). Embedding democratic imaginaries in shared norms and institutions challenges the politics of subordination. The radical democratic imaginary embraces pluralism and sees the importance for subordinated groups of working together while also retaining their autonomy. Smith (p 32) explains this achieves 'effective solidarity without asking any individual movement to pay the price of tokenism, co-optation and assimilation'. The good society is plural in character and yet preserves difference without leading to domination. French philosopher Jean-Luc Nancy (2001) calls this 'being singular plural'. He highlights the relational dimensions of 'being-together', 'being in common' and 'being-with' without collapsing the individual /identity into a totalising 'we' or collectivity.

Transgression

Transgressive Imaginations (O'Neill and Seal, 2012) explored the representation of criminalised and marginalised groups in fictive texts and arts-based ethnographic research. This involved deconstructing derogatory representations but also finding those which offer liberating and democratic potential. It took transgression – the breaking of boundaries and taboos – as its foundational concept. We drew on Jenks's (2003: 7) definition of transgression as 'a dynamic force in cultural production' and one which reveals the edges of collective order. Boundaries are crossed when individuals and groups are perceived to be 'out of place'. This boundary crossing might be purposeful on their part, or it might not. Instead, it might be a consequence of economic, social and cultural marginalisation. We emphasised that through challenging conformity, transgression can be liberating but that it can also entail facing punishment, censure or other forms of social and cultural exclusion. Those deemed transgressive against dominant norms do not necessarily embrace or even recognise this designation. Our intention was not to simply celebrate transgression as resistance in and of itself, but to unpack its effects in representations and lived experiences.

The other side of breaking boundaries is 'the reaffirmation of the shared values of the social order' (O'Neill and Seal, 2012: 5). Transgressing social and cultural norms ultimately helps to clarify and shore up boundaries. However, we stressed that social and cultural values are not settled or universally accepted. Examples of transgression – such as high-profile crimes – illustrate how such values are contentious and sites of struggle (Seal, 2010). They are also open to change. The boundaries of acceptability are not static, they shift over time and place; they are also different among different social groups.

Attention to the disturbance of social order also entails attention to social and cultural abjection. The abject does not respect rules and boundaries, but rather than directly contravening them, it is ambiguous and difficult to categorise. Abjection involves liminality and being inbetween – not clearly one thing or another (Van Gennep, 1960; Turner, 1967). This blurring of categories can induce disgust and attempts to banish the inbetween but it also inspires fascination and desire. Individuals and groups perceived to blur and mix categories of identity such as race, gender and sexuality are rendered abject. The interrelationship between disgust and desire means that the abject can evoke horror (Kristeva, 1982). Social prohibition depends on the intrusion of abject individuals and groups into the collective in order to clarify boundaries and to 'legitimize the prevailing order of power' (Tyler, 2013: 20). The abject is therefore essential to the dominant social imaginary (Stallybrass and White, 1986). Paradoxically, the objects of horror and disgust cannot be fully excluded from the social body and this offers the possibility of resistance – to the status of abjection and to oppressive power relations (Tyler, 2013).

In *Imaginative Criminology*, we build on our previous work but pay closer, more explicit attention to the spatialisation of transgression. This was not absent from *Transgressive Imaginations*; we addressed the othering of asylum seekers resulting from the 'protection' of national borders and the construction of Vancouver's skid row as a 'problem community' using mobile methods. However, we did not theorise transgression and space together, or develop our conceptual approach to space.

The significance of space, place and transgression

Cresswell (1996: 9) examines the intersection between our lived experiences of the world as 'a set of places' and transgression. Transgression 'serves to foreground the mapping of ideology onto space and place, and thus the margins can tell us something about "normality"' (p 9). When people are perceived as 'out of place', the normative assumptions and practices governing spatial inclusion and exclusion become apparent. The out of place, such as hippies congregating at Stonehenge and the women's peace camp at Greenham Common, become heretical (p 9). Campbell (2013: 22) analyses the 'politics of spatial meaning-making' in relation to the case of Wendy Lewis, a woman convicted of outraging public decency for urinating on the Blackpool cenotaph. Lewis was said to have defiled memorial space, revealing an 'imagined cartography of sacredness and purity' (p 31). In this book, we examine how imagined cartographies of space have rendered social groups abject through their expulsion from certain spaces and confinement in others. This includes Indigenous children who were removed from their families and placed in residential homes in 20th-century Australia, young women perceived as sexually transgressive confined in Magdalene laundries in Ireland, prisoners in contemporary England and Wales, and migrants and refugees contained in camps in various countries.

Work such as Campbell's (2013) demonstrates criminology's blossoming 'spatial turn'. More recently she has used 'assemblage thinking' to analyse the 'policing of bodies, space and things' in policing paedophilia through 'digital vigilantism' and reads this through *The Paedophile Hunter*, a made-for-television documentary (Campbell,

2016: 345). Hayward (2012: 441) argues that 'criminology has all too often taken space for granted'. Its history of attention to issues of power and meaning have 'only peripherally' engaged with spatiality. There are, of course, exceptions, as Campbell's work evidences. Criminology is witnessing increased engagement with spatialisation, particularly in relation to the contemporary city (Hayward, 2004; Kindynis, 2014), carceral geographies (Crewe et al, 2014; Moran, 2015) and mobile methods that engage with the kinaesthetic, transitory as well as material and affective dimensions of 'body and image-space' (Weigel, 1996; O'Neill, 2017). In this text we seek to further develop the relevance of meanings and experiences of space associated with practices of ordering. To do so, and in the spirit of imaginative criminology's intention to expand criminology's purview (Frauley, 2015a), we draw on insights gained from cultural geography, mobilities research and arts–based walking methods.

Imagining space

Lives are lived and felt in space. Space is culturally and socially constituted, and culture and social life are spatially situated and experienced (Lefebvre, 1991; Mitchell, 2000; Hubbard et al, 2002). Social and cultural phenomena cannot 'be torn from [their] spatial context' (Warf and Arias, 2009: 7). Lefebvre (1991) pinpoints the overemphasis of speech and writing in western notions of culture as meaning that the crucial role of space was traditionally overlooked. This has now changed with a discernible 'spatial turn' across many academic disciplines (Warf and Arias, 2009). Discourses of space are 'central to our everyday conceptions of ourselves and reality' (Shields, 1991: 7). The social and cultural production of space means that it is plural and interrelational (Massey, 2005). Lived spaces are polysemic; there is no single vision or experience of a given space. Instead, there is a joining up of different pasts, presents and futures (Bailly, 1993), and always more than one story going on at once (Massey, 1999). This conception of space leads Massey (2005) to argue that space should not be understood simply as a surface on which things happen. Rather, it is a meeting of histories. This notion of histories meeting is significant to most of our examples, from the way encounters between white settlers and Indigenous people have shaped the Australian landscape; to the traces of historical punishment in the modern city observed during a ghost walk in Durham; to the continued spatialising effects of the 'peace lines' and 'border lines' resulting from war and conflict in present-day Belfast.

Space exists in the imagination and as a concrete reality (Shields, 1991), although its multiple symbolisms mean that this is not a clear binary (Bailly, 1993; Rose, 1996). The ways in which space is imagined, and the meanings that it has, shape the experience of the concrete reality. The contemporary significance of virtual space underlines how space does not necessarily connote a physical surface, or require the separation of real and imagined (Warf and Arias, 2009). Lefebvre (1991) draws on Bataille to argue that there is a conjunction between inner lives and physical spaces – and this conjunction can also apply to spaces that do not have a physical surface. The imaginary relations between the self and other are performed in space (Rose, 1996). Imagined, or in Lefebvre's (1991) terms, 'representational', spaces are lived through 'associated images and symbols' (p 39). They 'need obey no rules of consistency or cohesiveness' (p 41) and have centres of affective meaning. Representations of space in personal testimony, film, arts and fictive texts are examined across all of our chapters. We embrace the notion of space as both lived and imagined, without a clear separation existing between the two. In Chapter 7, we turn our attention to imagined alternative worlds through analysis of young adult dystopian fiction.

The interconnection of space, meaning and feeling highlights its significance to cultural and individual memory (Bailly, 1993). Particular spaces, such as one's childhood home, are experienced in thought and dreams. Our memories, and our intimate lives, are housed but our memories and dreams are of spaces which have also gone (Bachelard, 1994). Bachelard (p xxxv) emphasises the human value of loved spaces, which he terms 'eulogized space'. This is a powerful notion and one that is interconnected with memories of space and spaces of memorialisation. However, the multiple histories of space mean that such memories are contested and polysemic (Bailly, 1993). Sites have fragmented and convoluted histories (de Certeau, 1985). Some spaces are remembered as loved; others are remembered as sites of trauma. Many will bear these different histories simultaneously. Memories of space, both troubling and sustaining, are central to our analysis in relation to confinement in residential schools, Magdalene laundries, prisons and camps. Individual recollections of loved spaces in unlikely settings underline the complexity and ambivalence of both space and memory. Contested collective memories of space are especially pertinent to Chapter 6's exploration of both the Women's Memorial March in Downtown Vancouver and the peace lines and border walls of Belfast. These examples trenchantly illustrate spatial history as polysemic, traumatic and involving political struggle.

Particular spaces can have socially sanctioned roles and meanings, such as for work, play or worship (Lefebvre, 1991). As discussed previously, when these roles and meanings are transgressed, whether intentionally or not, two things happen. One is that the boundaries around certain spaces are clarified; the other is that certain people and groups are constructed as abject to those spaces. There are also zones of prohibition, which are defined by what is banned (Lefebvre, 1991). Bancroft (2012: 64) explores the spatial restrictions placed on 'social crimes' such as homelessness and sex work in American cities to make 'links between space, power and social control'. Boundaries are both political and policed, creating geographies of dominance that define who is let in and who is kept out (Mitchell, 2000; Hubbard et al, 2002). Mitchell (2000) gives the example of racial segregation as highlighting the spatial reproduction of hegemony. The spatial imaginary is shaped by dominant discourses of gender, race, nationality and class (Rose, 1996; Domosh, 1998; Mitchell, 2000). The reshaping of the Australian landscape according to a white settler imaginary is one such example of the spatial reproduction of racialised hegemony; the confinement of refugees and migrants in the liminal, extranational spaces of camps is a pertinent example of how geographies of dominance interact with imagined national communities.

Space is constituted through 'maps of power' but it is also contested and disrupted (Massey, 1999: 11). There are geographies of dominance but also geographies of transgression and resistance (Hubbard et al, 2002). The Women's Memorial March in Downtown Vancouver protests at the indifference to the disappearances and murders of women, disproportionate numbers of whom are sex workers and Indigenous. The protest is led by women traditionally subject to the spatial restriction of 'social crimes' described above. Political struggle is 'inscribed in space' (Lefebvre, 1991: 55). De Certeau (1985: 127) examines how the management of the contemporary city as orderly space entails the attempt to eliminate 'garbage' – of 'abnormality, deviance, and sickness'. However, the city is 'impossible to manage' and its denizens employ tricks and tactics – small, barely visible acts – to subvert the topographic system (p 128). One of these means of subversion is walking. Walkers generate their own routes and transform planned and regulated spaces into something else. They create discontinuities which 'play [...] with spatial organisations, however panoptic' (p 136). Walking enables the exploration of memory in sites 'haunted by countless ghosts that lurk there in silence to be "evoked" or not' (p 143). As Gordon (1997: 203) argues, attention to 'ghostly matters' – the illumination 'of things not seen, neglected and banished' – is crucial to the sociological imagination.

Domosh (1998) employs de Certeau's (1985) notion of tactics to uncover everyday transgressions of space in 19th-century New York, such as fashionable, middle class women who were out in the city at the 'wrong' time. These micropolitical acts of transgression need our attention in order to 'adequately describe the complexities of real life' (p 210). Micropolitics is the 'barely perceived transitions in power that occur in and through situated encounters' (Bissell, 2016: 397). Such transitions take place from moment to moment but are entangled with structural, macropolitical power differences. The history of walking is also deeply connected to social and structural differences, and the politics of race, gender and social class as expressed in the work of Engels, Mayhew and Orwell. While the 19th-century male 'flâneur' was writing about taking tortoises for a walk as an expression of resistance to modernity and the acceleration of social life, in interwar Britain Virginia Woolf needed the excuse of shopping for a pencil to venture out and walk in public as an upper middle class woman. The Vagrancy Acts of 1824 and the formation of modern police in London in 1829 aimed to 'oversee' the street and police the poor, while the Contagious Diseases Acts (1864, 1866 and 1869) aimed to protect the nation's (men's) health while at the same time policing 'poor' women and the urban underclasses (Walkowitz 1980).

Walking is something we do every day, yet reflect on little. There is a long history of walking in arts practice including the work of Heddon (2008), Hind and Qualmann (2015), Long (1967), and Fulton (2010), as well as in ethnography and anthropology (Edensor, 2010; Ingold and Vergunst 2008; and Pink, 2007) with some work in biographical sociology and criminology (O'Neill and Hubbard, 2010; O'Neill and Stenning, 2014; O'Neill and Roberts, 2019). A good example of urban and micropolitical transgression challenging and resisting gendered norms is articulated in the arts practice of a collective of women walking artists, 'walkwalkwalk'. In re-examining their routine walks in the city, they discovered that as the project developed it had the effect of 'tracking some of the changes that were happening in the city ... as the East London Line extension' was in construction alongside the redevelopment, regeneration and gentrification of the area. As part of the project they undertook walks at night, including perambulator walks; with their children in pushchairs and prams they walked in places they might not feel comfortable in during the day. Setting up braziers, making food and soup, and inhabiting those places in a different way, they took hold of space and places and found that this had the effect of changing the way they felt in those places. Qualmann says they all

> shared feelings of anxiety about unpromising looking dark alley ways, yet when we did some flyposting – using stories that we'd written from encounters along the walk and putting them back onto the route, changed the way we felt .... but the main thing is it's a shift in mentality or psychology of your behaviour within the space and through that process, claiming it and feeling safe and I think once you repeat that and nothing bad happens you do start to feel safe, and like you have a right to the space. (Qualmann and O'Neill, 2017:np)

A focus on walking in criminological research raises awareness of the researcher as a moving, interacting, relational being, in and through space and place, in the context of a criminology that is 'on the move'. Walking-based research follows other 'innovations' in research methods such as digital and multi-modal research and is inspired by the various 'turns' in sociological and criminological research – such as the cultural, narrative, visual/sensory, performative and mobile. Walking research also enables analysis of capitalist and neoliberal spaces. In the walks discussed in Chapters 5 and 6 we get a sense of the shifts and changes in city spaces, the regeneration and gentrification of the Downtown Eastside in Vancouver and the removal or 'cleansing' of the poor, infirm and homeless. In a walking interview with Kerry Porth the sensory, multi-modal and political impact of regeneration, gentrification and redevelopment is felt in Vancouver's Downtown Eastside, such that a biography of place is told in the walk undertaken.

Massey (2005) argues that the way in which space is imagined has effects, and notes that 'space' and 'place' have been dichotomised, with space representing the abstract and place the everyday and 'real'. She argues against this dialectic in order to recognise the multiple trajectories of space and to resist false equivalences such as 'everyday' and 'local'. Massey (2005) outlines three ways to conceptualise the 'connections between the imagination of the spatial and the imagination of the political' (p 10). First, conceiving of space as interrelational chimes well with anti-essentialist politics, which take identities to be constructed and interrelational and resonates with radical democratic pluralism. Second, space as a sphere of multiplicity allies with the concern to replace single stories and histories with many. Third, 'imagining space as always in process' is related to an insistence 'on the genuine openness of the future' (p 11). The terms of the openness and closure of space must be interrogated; she asks, 'Against what are boundaries erected?' (p 180). If space is imagined as plural, multiple and unfinished, the future is left open. This is crucial for radical democratic politics and imagining new worlds (Massey, 1999). Foucault (1986) conceptualises spaces of multiplicity, difference and inversion as heterotopias – counter-sites that disturb and unsettle and are 'starting point[s] for imagining, inventing and diversifying space' (Johnson, 2013: 800).

The spatial imaginary is central to the analyses and arguments in this book. Via attention to a range of different imagined spaces, we highlight the spatialisation of transgression and practices of exclusion, but also resistance and the promise and possibility of counter-sites of diversity. We also highlight how lives are lived, experienced and told in these spaces.

We explore a heterogeneous range of topics and approaches as examples of ways of doing imaginative criminology. This is in keeping with our politics of radical democratic pluralism. It is also necessary as there is no single or best way to do imaginative criminology; there is a multiplicity of ways. However, in addition to the imaginary, transgression and space there are some other key concepts that guide our analysis across the different chapters and act as threads linking the topics to one another.

We consider different spaces of **confinement** and understand these as sites characterised by regimes of power/knowledge, discipline and resistance, and control and care, while paying attention to how the experience of confinement shapes subjectivity and states of being (Jefferson, 2014). The significance and operation of **borders** in relation to practices of spatial control is another key concept. Space is bounded according to legal territories, which has profound consequences for citizenship and the exercise of rights. As such, borders are 'manifestations of power' (Diener and Hagan, 2012: 121). They also operate at micro-levels of spatial organisation such as different zones within particular cities, or within institutions. The borders and boundaries around 'a delineated collectivity, that includes some people – concrete or not – and excludes others, involves an act of active imagination' (Yuval-Davis and Stoetzler, 2002: 331). The concepts of **memory** and **cultural memory** are also of crucial importance as memory is an essential component of social, group and individual imaginaries. Memory is produced and reproduced socially, culturally and spatially, but is also mediated by individual experience. To make sense of the past, 'people draw on their individual experiences and the wider social context' (Seal, 2014:

167). Cultural memory refers to the shared memories of groups and societies that are constructed through cultural products and media representations (Molloy, 2015).

Methodologically, our analytic approach is avowedly critical, historical and cultural, using mixed, constellational, creative, participatory methods, ethnography and walking (ethno-mimetic) as a way of both knowing, understanding and doing criminological research; as a kinaesthetic, spatial, imaginative mobile criminology for the 21st century. This distinctive mix of methods characterises our approach. Listening to the experiences of people seeking safety, using ethnographic, biographical and artistic methods, and focusing attention on the **micrology** of lived experience – the minutiae, the small scale – we can often reach a better understanding of the larger picture. As Adorno (1978: 50) said, 'the splinter in your eye is the best magnifying glass', meaning that focusing on the 'micrology' of lived experience can often shed light on broader structures, relationships, discourses and processes that are not only the outcome but the medium of social action and meaning making.

In Chapter 2 we examine historical confinement via the example of homes for Indigenous children in Australia. Between 1910 and 1970 Indigenous children were removed from their families and placed in children's homes in order to assimilate and 'civilise' them. Frequently, this removal was forcible. This chapter explores how these homes are remembered and imagined in oral history testimonies, as well as in the cultural representations, *Follow the Rabbit Proof Fence* ([2002] 2013), Doris Garimara Pilkington's life narrative, and its film adaptation, *Rabbit Proof Fence* (Noyce, 2002). The spaces of these confining institutions have not received full attention from criminologists; however, these were crucial sites of social control and human rights abuses.

Building on the idea of memory explored in Chapter 2, Chapter 3 turns its attention to memories of the Magdalene Laundries in Ireland, which housed poor and 'deviant' young women. It draws on feminist history to explore the laundries as sites of gendered social control and analyses the reconstruction of these spaces in oral histories and the documentary *Witness: Sex in a Cold Climate* (Channel 4, 1998), and their portrayal in the films *The Magdalene Sisters* (Mullan, 2002) and *Philomena* (Frears, 2013). Concepts of memory, including forgetting and rediscovery – at individual, familial and national levels – are utilised.

Chapter 4 discusses two creative writing projects with male prisoners in HM Prisons Lewes and Durham. Here we examine methodological issues associated with the relevance of space and setting to participatory arts (PA) research in prison, and the imaginative writing produced by participants. Memories, relationships, and the experience of 'inside' and 'outside' were all significant features of prisoners' writing. This writing is read not simply as 'research data' but also as creative and cultural expression. The Lewes project involved using texts from the Mass Observation Archive as inspiration for prisoners' poetry (see Davey, 2015). Themes of creative writing, history and criminal justice are taken up in relation to the Durham project in which creative writing groups 'inside' and 'outside' Durham prison wrote ghost stories based on the prison and the history of crime and punishment in the city. This is explored in this chapter, along with a crime walk that was developed as part of the project, which serves as an example of public criminology. In discussing both projects we reflect on how walking, combined with PA, 'can be a way of both *knowing* and *understanding* the history of crime, justice, punishment in city spaces' (O'Neill and Hill, no date).

Continuing the focus on space and place in imaginative criminology, Chapter 5, 'Border spaces and places: the age of the camps', discusses arts-based research (filmic analysis and walking ethnographies) with asylum seekers and migrants waiting in border spaces, mostly in camps (in Greece, France, Jordan and Melilla) to move on with their journey. The construction of the camp as a site of containment, constraint and a border space and what this means in the lives of the people and families waiting, some for many years, is examined through narrative interviews, photographs and filmic work. We examine the constitution of space through the relational, embodied and imagined experiences of migrants and the material and symbolic concept of the border and border spaces in their lives, journeys and sense of belonging.

In Chapter 6 we focus specifically on the issue of space, place, violence and transgression drawing on case studies in Canada and Northern Ireland. 'Imagining spaces of violence and transgression in Vancouver and Northern Ireland' focuses first of all on the lives of Indigenous women and sex workers in Vancouver's Downtown Eastside (DTES). For 26 years, on 14 February, Valentine's Day, women of the DTES have led a memorial march through the city, stopping at the places and spaces where women were murdered or went missing. We draw on material from walking methods, participatory photographs and interviews with women who attended the march in 2016 to examine spaces of past, present and future in their lives. Continuing the theme of the construction and impact of space and borders explored in the previous chapter, this chapter also examines the history of the 'peace walls', 'peace lines' or 'border lines' in Belfast in the context of spaces of war, violence and conflict in Northern Ireland. Specifically the 'architecture of conflict' is explored through criminological scholarship on the conflict in Northern Ireland. As with the Vancouver case study, arts-based walking methods are utilised that explore these border spaces through sensory, kinaesthetic, multi-modal research with citizens of Belfast.

In Chapter 7, 'Imagining dystopian futures in young adult fiction', we discuss how it is notable that 'speculative fiction' – fiction that creates alternative worlds – frequently addresses themes of deviance, transgression and ordering. Here we discuss the exploration of themes of surveillance and spectacular punishment; hyperreality and virtual reality; memory and the suppression of history; and hierarchy and difference in dystopian fiction aimed at young adults – *The Hunger Games* (Collins, 2008), *The Maze Runner* (Dashner, 2009), *Divergent* (Roth, 2011) and *Red Rising* (Brown, 2014). We explore the role of this fiction in cultural imaginings of social control, repression and resistance, and argue for greater criminological attention to novels, including bestselling fiction.

Finally, in our concluding chapter, we reflect on how the theoretical and methodological threads running through book tie together to develop an imaginative criminology of space. Building on previous calls for the importance of 'imaginative criminology' (Carlen, 2010; 2017; Young, 2011; Frauley, 2015a), including the use of creative methodologies (Walklate and Jacobsen, 2017), and our previous work towards a radical democratic imaginary, we argue that an imaginative approach is necessary in order to comprehend the complexity of issues of transgression and space, and to ensure the continued reinvigoration of criminology as a discipline.

Historical Spaces of Confinement 1: Homes for Indigenous Children in Australia

Cultural criminologists have interrogated the representation of prisons in the popular imagination but other spaces of confinement have received far less criminological attention (see Rafter, 2006; Brown, 2009). Brown (2009: 5) contends that representations of prison operate as a cultural resource for people to make sense of punishment and provide 'frameworks for ordinary citizens to step into or out of self-conscious modes of awareness as moral spectators and deliberative citizens'. This approach can be applied to representations of other spaces of confinement, which were not prisons but were a 'barrier to social intercourse with the outside and to departure' (Goffman, [1961] 2007: 4). This is the first of two chapters that focus on imagining space in institutions that were based on confinement and control, but were not penal: homes for Indigenous children in Australia and Magdalene laundries in Ireland. Different types of representation of historical confinement highlight the significance of memory and cultural memory and enable making sense of and thinking through these institutions.

In focusing on how spaces of confinement are imagined, we employ Goffman's ([1961] 2007) work on total institutions. As Scott (2010) argues, the spatial organisation of confining institutions was crucial to their regimes. They physically confined inmates and limited their access to resources. Along with prisons, Goffman ([1961] 2007) identified hospitals, army barracks and boarding schools as examples of total institutions. They all segregated disorderly groups from mainstream society and sought to reform and improve them. This attention to measures for dealing with the disorderly is highly relevant to our focus on transgression and the social control of those perceived to disturb order. Goffman's exploration of inmates' small successes within the total institution, which allowed them to retain a sense of independence, and their ways of 'making do' anticipated later work on the micropolitics of resistance (Scott, 2010). Although criticised for neglecting issues of power, Scott (2011) contends that Goffman's focus on coercion, dominance and hierarchy in total institutions, which are 'forcing houses for changing persons' (Goffman, [1961] 2007: 22), demonstrates that the negotiation of power is central to the concept.

Another reason for employing the concept of the total institution is that it has resonated beyond academic social science, meaning that it has helped to shape some cultural representations and cultural memory of confinement. Erving Goffman's books sold well and he had a readership among the general public as well as academics (Ritzer, 1998). He has influenced writers such as Alan Bennett, who expressed his appreciation of Goffman's work in the *London Review of Books* (Bennett, 1981). Patrick McGrath's novel *Spider* (1990), which was adapted into a film directed by David Cronenberg (2002), partly drew on *Asylums* (Goffman, [1961] 2007) and the concept of the total institution for its depiction of the protagonist's incarceration in a secure mental hospital (Honigmann, 1991). The portrayals of residential schools and Magdalene laundries that we explore bear the influence of the notion of the total institution. This exemplifies Rafter and Brown's (2011: 1) argument that 'criminology is hard at work in culture and that culture is hard at work in criminology'. They explain that interpretations of social phenomena such as crime and transgression in cultural forms coincide with academic work. Interpretations of total institutionalisation as they appear in cultural representations and oral history testimonies demonstrate this interchange quite clearly.

Cunneen and Tauri (2016: 11) argue that as a discipline, criminology has been largely silent on the crimes and harms of settler colonialism, which 'is itself an effect of colonialism'. In this chapter, we consider the forms of imaginative criminology that permit attention to these harms. Through analysis of Doris Garimara Pilkington's life narrative *Follow the Rabbit Proof Fence* (2002), its film adaptation *Rabbit Proof Fence* (Dir Noyce, 2002) and 12 oral history interviews, this chapter examines representations and memories of the constellation of orphanages, children's homes and dormitories in which Indigenous children were placed after being removed from their families in early and mid 20th-century Australia. All of these sources portray the experiences of real individuals, although as creative non-fiction, film and oral history testimonies, they take very different forms. In triangulating them, we adopt O'Neill's (1998: 128) approach of finding interrelations between diverse texts and of regarding them as 'powerful learning tools'. They constitute 'feeling forms' that engage audiences with the 'the affects, sentiments and experiences of marginalized peoples' and can promote a 'politics of feeling' (O'Neill, 2001: 54). Considered together, the sources are frameworks for 'ordinary citizens' to comprehend the devastating impacts of white settler colonial domination, but also the multiple ways in which this was lived, survived and resisted by Indigenous people.

Child removal and the stolen generations in Australia

By the 1930s, the state was the legal guardian of nearly all Indigenous children in Australia. The construction of a 'legislative apparatus' for the 'protection' of these children built on the existing 'social technology' of rescue and discipline that European churches and state agencies had historically employed in relation to the children of the poor (van Krieken, 1999a: 302). Racist fears that Indigenous people posed a threat to 'white civilisation', particularly through racial mixing and the birth of 'half caste' children, underpinned policies of forcible removal that were enacted to bring about the assimilation of Indigenous children into 'European' society. Colonialist and welfarist discourses intertwined to justify children's removal from their families and communities as being in their best interests (van Krieken, 1999a; 1999b). Cunneen and Tauri (2016: 54) state that '[p]rotection was based on a penal model of administration and control' as it was rule bound and coercive. For example, Indigenous people living on reserves needed the (white) superintendent's permission in order to leave.

The Inquiry into the Separation of Aboriginal and Torres Strait Islander Children from their Families was launched in 1995, initiated by Michael Lavarch, the Australian Attorney General at the time. It published its findings in the 'Bringing Them Home' report of 1997, which was based on evidence taken from 535 Indigenous people (Chandra-Shekeran, 1998; Cunneen, 1999). 'Bringing Them Home' argued that forcible removal constituted cultural genocide, defined by the 1948 UN Convention on the Prevention and Punishment of the Crime of Genocide as including the transfer of children from one group to another group, with the aim of destroying that group (van Krieken, 1999a). The report made 54 recommendations, including the need for reparation in the form of compensation and apology (Chandra-Shekeran, 1998; Cunneen, 1999). Labour Prime Minister Kevin Rudd made an official apology to the Stolen Generations in 2008, following 11 years of refusal by his Liberal predecessor, John Howard (Cuthbert and Quartly, 2013). The recommended Reparations Tribunal was not established and the federal government has not awarded financial compensation, although there have been state-level schemes in South Australia, Tasmania and New South Wales (Cunneen, 2016; Whitbourn 2016).

Doris Garimara Pilkington's life narrative, *Follow the Rabbit Proof Fence*, was originally published in 1996. The context of the publication of 'Bringing Them Home' is highly relevant to how it has been interpreted and understood (Molloy, 2015). Its cinematic adaptation, *Rabbit Proof Fence*, was released in 2002, five years after the 'Bringing Them Home' report, and is 'one of the few Stolen Generations narratives to circulate internationally' (Kennedy, 2008: 167). These texts help to form the basis of cultural memory of forcible child removal; one which is of course deeply contested. Cultural memory is 'the shared memories or remembrances of groups ... produced by public, mediated representations of the past' (Molloy, 2015: viii). It is not static, but is 'in a process of perpetual motion' (p ix).

The Bringing Them Home Oral History Project was established in order to meet the first recommendation of the report, which was to 'record, preserve and administer access to testimonies of Indigenous people affected by the forcible removal policies' (Bringing Them Home, 1997). As such, the testimonies have been gathered as part of the state-mandated effort to attempt to confront the traumatic history of child removal and to record 'a more democratised version of history' (Mellor and Haebich, 2002: 10). Along with cultural texts such as memoirs, novels and films, they form the cultural memory of the Stolen Generations. A pilot project in 1998, followed by a full project commencing in 1999, collected 340 oral history interviews from people who had experienced removal to children's homes and also from people who worked in them.

Children's homes as spaces of confinement

Jefferson (2014: 45) defines confining institutions as 'sites where social power is a central dynamic and where practices of power and knowledge, discipline and resistance, control and care are key features'. Children's homes for Indigenous children in Australia clearly met this definition. They were intended not only for control and care, but also to strip children of their Indigenous identities (Choo, 2002). Different confining sites can resemble one another in terms of their practices and how they are experienced (Goffman, [1961] 2007; Jefferson, 2014). This does not mean that they are the same as one another; children's homes were not prisons, although they shared certain features with them.

Chiming with Foucault's (1979) concept of the gulag archipelago, Clark (2002: 165) describes the network of Australian institutions in which Indigenous children were placed as 'tiny islands scattered across the continent'. These were both separate from mainstream Australian white settler life and the dominant social imaginary but also an integral part of it. States such as New South Wales had children's homes specifically for Indigenous children and Western Australia had homes for 'nearly white' children; states with fewer Indigenous people placed children in mainstream children's homes and orphanages, as well as with white foster families. Children's homes were not uniform in terms of their regimes or the extent to which their residents participated in the wider community. Some regimes were based mainly on doing chores, whereas others provided more recreation time. Children from certain homes attended mainstream local schools (Clark, 2002).

The regimes and practices of confining institutions have implications for the subjectivity and states of being of those who experience them (Jefferson, 2014). It is necessary to examine how such practices were experienced and the meanings that they generated. The ways in which children's homes have been represented and imagined contribute to recognising the harms of colonial domination. The analysis of the portrayals of child removal in this chapter specifically focuses on understanding the significance of children's homes as sites of confinement.

Follow the Rabbit Proof Fence (Garimara Pilkington, 2002)

Garimara Pilkington's (2002) life narrative is the story of how her mother Molly and two aunts Daisy and Gracie escaped from the government mission for Indigenous children to which they had been forcibly removed and journeyed home by finding their way to and following the rabbit-proof fence that crosses Western Australia. It is based on interviews about events from the 1930s, which Garimara Pilkington carried out with the three women when they were in their 60s and 70s. As such, it offers an affective narrative based on personal experience as well as a situated history of child removal. Orality and memory are crucial to telling the story, which Klein (2016) argues gives non-Indigenous readers the opportunity to engage with Indigenous customs and history as a counter imaginary to colonial dominance. Kennedy (2008) notes that as Garimara Pilkington was herself a removed child, she occupied the hybrid position of outsider and insider in relation to both Indigenous and white settler cultures.

Follow the Rabbit Proof Fence contextualises forcible child removal and the story of three girls' journey in relation to the history of colonialism, white settlement and dispossession from the land (Kennedy, 2008). The initial five chapters detail the history of this dispossession, from the rapacious first contact between white raiders and Indigenous societies in what would become Western Australia, to the arrival of European settlers in 1829 and the completion of the 1,834 kilometre rabbit-proof fence in 1907. This was the point at which a base camp for the fence's maintenance men was established at Jigalong. By the 1930s, Jigalong was a site for 'sacred and secret ceremonies' for Indigenous people and also home to Molly, Daisy and Gracie (Garimara Pilkington, 2002: 35). This historical context related in the narrative's opening chapters emphasises that the Australian landmass is a polysemic space with multiple histories that meet and diverge at key points such as Jigalong, and about which there are numerous stories (Bailly, 1993; Massey, 1999; 2005). Molly's mother Maude was an Indigenous woman and her father was the white boss of the base camp. Daisy and Gracie also had Indigenous mothers and white fathers. Due to the girls' mixed heritage,[1] the Chief Protector of Aborigines for Western Australia recommended their removal from Jigalong to the Moore River Native Settlement hundreds of kilometres away.

As Klein (2016: 599) argues, Garimara Pilkington employs prison imagery and similes to evoke the Settlement, situating forced removal 'in the context of criminal justice'. After the girls' arrival there, Molly reflects that 'It's like a gaol. They lock you up at night time and come and open the door in the morning'. The girls 'all noticed the bars across the windows and were really scared of them' (Garimara Pilkington, 2002: 66). This prison-like environment induces in Molly 'a deep longing for the dry, rugged, red landscape of the Pilbara', the contrasting open landscape of her home (p 66). The girls sleep on cyclone beds (camp beds with mesh frames) in overcrowded dormitories that have wire screens and iron bars on the windows. The narrative states that '[i]t looked more like a concentration camp than a residential school' (p 72). In evoking the concentration camp, Garimara Pilkington emphasises the Settlement as a space of confinement but also underlines its relationship with preceding spaces of colonial confinement and forcible resettlement, and the genocide of the Holocaust (on the history of concentration camps, see Stone, 2017).

A detached concrete room with a sand floor known as 'the boob' is used to punish children for infractions such as swearing at teachers and running away, with some incarcerated in it for up to 14 days. Other punishments include being restricted to bread and water and 'gestures of humiliation' such as head shaving (Goffman, [1961] 2007: 22). The prison comparisons extend beyond the spatial environment of the school to the nature of the daily regime. The children are inmates rather than students. They are forbidden from using their own

---

[1] 'Mixed' was a white colonialist designation.

languages and must instead speak only in English. The Moore River Settlement is portrayed in the text as similar to a carceral institution; one which realises the ideology of separation and assimilation of mixed heritage children propagated by white settler elites and which is the instrument of cultural genocide.

Molly resolves to escape from Moore River after listening to 'the slide of the bolt and the rattle of the padlock' as the children are locked in the dormitory for the night (Garimara Pilkington, 2002: 74). She, Daisy and Gracie run away and begin the massive journey back to Jigalong. Their walk across the openness of the landscape of Western Australia contrasts with their incarceration at Moore River. They travel through 'a wide area of coastal, sandy heaths and had the pleasure to see a variety of flowers' (p 84) and the 'sounds of fowls, squeaky windmills and barking dogs' remind them of home (p 97). The girls are resourceful and unafraid in the wilderness; they catch rabbits to eat and make shelters for the night. Their skilfulness and capability is a rebuke to the colonialist discourses of protection and 'civilisation' that underpinned forcible child removal. While extracts from official documents such as police reports inserted into the text reveal that the authorities were outwitted by the girls and were unable to recapture them during their trek, Garimara Pilkington describes how 'The absconders gleaned all the positive energy from the environment, from everything that lived and breathed around them' (p 109).

Finding the rabbit-proof fence enables the girls to orientate themselves properly for their journey back to Jigalong. The fence is on the one hand a spatial metaphor of colonial domination (Cain, 2004), which symbolises and helps to enact the occupation of the white settlers and the colonial practices that breached 'familial, communal and place-based ties' of Indigenous people (Lovrod, 2015: 72). It is a master symbol of colonial geography and exemplifies the use of boundaries – both physical and imagined – for racialised social control, subjugation and ordering. However, by providing Molly, Daisy and Gracie with a map home, it facilitates a resistant geography and subversion of colonialist ideology (Lovrod, 2015; Klein, 2016). The girls' achievement in overcoming white authoritarian control is heroic. Garimara Pilkington states that over nine weeks the girls 'trekked across it [the outback] and conquered it' (p 130).

The girls did not, however, escape colonialist control. Gracie was captured and sent back to the Moore River Settlement after deciding to take a train to Wiluna to find her mother instead of completing the walk to Jigalong. In the final chapter of the narrative, we learn that in 1940, after getting married and having two daughters, Molly was again sent to Moore River. She returned to Jigalong following the same route as when she was a child, taking one daughter, Annabelle, with her. Doris, the author, remained in the institution. Three years later, Annabelle was removed and Molly never saw her again. The text does not end with redemption but with repeated trauma (Beyer, 2010; Klein, 2016). Nevertheless, the girls' heroic escape and long journey across the wilderness leaves an indelible impression on the reader. The life narrative is a learning tool and feeling form in that it helps readers to comprehend the lived experience of removal and confinement in relation the Stolen Generations and creates a politics of feeling in its affective illustration of the harms of colonial domination as enacted through space and geography.

Rabbit Proof Fence (Noyce, 2002)

The film *Rabbit Proof Fence*, directed by Philip Noyce, is an adaptation of Garimara Pilkington's narrative and post-dates 'Bringing Them Home'. Kennedy (2008) notes that the cultural memory of the Stolen Generations that the film conveys is mediated through the conventions of transnational discourses of trauma, particularly those associated with representations of the Holocaust. As in *Schindler's List* (Dir Spielberg, 1993) one particular story stands for the multitude of stories of the Stolen Generations. In this sense, the film explicitly sets out to epitomise the cultural memory of forcible child removal nationally and, as it was also made for international audiences, transculturally (see Garde-Hansen, 2011). The film portrays the removal of the three girls, their time at Moore River and their journey home. Unlike *Follow the Rabbit Proof Fence*, with its chapters detailing colonial settlement, the film's narrative begins in 1931. It opens with captions that situate the events in Western Australia and which explain that the Aborigine Act controlled the lives of Indigenous people, including enabling the removal of 'half caste' children. It draws authority from Molly's voiceover, which states 'This is a true story'.

The opening scenes contrast the camp at Jigalong, which is surrounded by a wide, scrubby landscape and is home to the three girls, with the city streets of Perth, busy with people and cars. This is the location of A O Neville, the Chief Protector of Aborigines, who is depicted making decisions about his charges' lives, from whether they can buy new shoes to whether they can marry. It is he who authorises the removal of Molly, Gracie and Daisy to the Moore River Settlement. These scenes establish a set of binaries represented in the film: white/black, European/Indigenous, 'civilised'/'uncivilised', which Cain (2004) argues seek to incorporate otherness. Once the binaries that supported colonial ideology and practice, in *Rabbit Proof Fence* they underpin 'postcolonial settler anxiety' about Australia's colonial past – an anxiety that mourns the past but frequently does not acknowledge the ongoing harms of white settler domination (Cain, 2004: 303; Kennedy, 2008).

The traumatic kidnap of the three girls from their home, during which they are forcibly grabbed from their mothers and bundled into a car as the women of Jigalong grieve, is followed by a scene in which Chief Protector Neville gives a eugenics-based lecture. He explains that such removals are designed to 'breed out' bad blood and that institutions such as the Moore River Settlement have 'the benefit of everything our culture has to offer'. This juxtaposition highlights the binaries around which the film is constructed but also which it aims to expose and critique – in particular, colonialist assumptions that the superiority of 'European' civilisation meant the inevitable disappearance of Indigenous culture (see van Krieken, 1999a).

Taking its lead from Garimara Pilkington's use of prison imagery, the depiction of Moore River in the film emphasises its role as a space of confinement that operates according to an institutional regime reminiscent of prison or an army barracks. Molly, Gracie and Daisy arrive there at night and are taken to a crowded dormitory full of army-style cots for the children to sleep on. They are woken in the morning by a stick knocking on the outside of the building and have to get up to make their beds. Their accommodation is a cottage-type wooden house in a row of other cottages. They are forbidden from talking in the dining room and also from using languages other than English. The children are shown engaged in chores such as sweeping up and their time is managed by bells ringing. A returned runaway girl is punished in front of the other children with a beating, highlighting the punitive aspects of the Settlement's regime.

Molly, Gracie and Daisy escape from Moore River while everyone else is at a church located in the centre of the two rows of wooden cottages in which the children are housed, and make their way through the woods as a storm breaks. Their journey through the open grassland of the outback is intercut with scenes of Neville in his Perth office, surrounded by the trappings of modernity such as wooden filing cabinets, his telephone and the maps with which he attempts to find them. His putative superiority is satirised, both in relation to colonialist assumptions as to white people's greater intelligence and capability, and in relation to the assumed superiority of bureaucracy-bound 'European' culture. Neville is depicted largely within low-lit confined spaces such as the office and the lecture hall, suggesting continuities between different institutional spaces of modernity.

The girls evade the tracker sent to follow them and navigate their way through changing scenery, guided by the rabbit-proof fence. The trope of the fence visually and spatially symbolises the divisions between, and the parameters of, two different sets of cultural norms (Cain, 2004). Land, as Cain (p 300) argues, is a dominant feature in the film, which maps the outback as 'an encounter between two different cultures'. As such, it acknowledges more than one history. Aerial shots show the girls crossing a vast arid landscape, their resourcefulness and knowledge of how to survive the terrain leaving Neville out-manoeuvred and outwitted, despite his supposed 'civilisation'.

After Gracie is captured at a railway station, Molly and Daisy wearily continue their walk back to Jigalong, Molly sometimes carrying Daisy. Once home they run to Maude, Molly's mother. Kennedy (2008: 170) argues that the film employs elements of maternal melodrama but also 'acknowledges the limits of translating trauma across cultural difference'. The real Molly Kelly's voiceover situates the trauma as part of Indigenous experience that results from the cruelties of Western colonialism (Lovrod, 2015). Her voice subverts the happy, Hollywood-style ending of Molly and Daisy's emotional reunion with Maude. She informs viewers that her own daughters were taken from her and that Gracie never came back home to Jigalong.

The film's final captions inform/remind viewers that Indigenous children were removed from their families until 1970 – years past the particular story they have just witnessed. Cain (2004) argues that on the one hand, *Rabbit Proof Fence* indulges white settler guilt by inviting white viewers to identify with the Indigenous characters, while maintaining a sense of the characters' otherness from the dominant social imaginary. However, she also emphasises that its focus on the destructive nature of colonial policies of child removal 'stands in contrast to the political refusal [at the time] of the Australian Government to acknowledge the fact of the "stolen generation"' (p 303). This counter-narrative creates an opening for a radical democratic imaginary. *Rabbit Proof Fence* is a cultural resource for non-Indigenous audiences to make sense of child removal and confinement in children's homes and offers a framework for them to be deliberative citizens about its ongoing impacts. It does not create the same degree of affective understanding as Garimara Pilkington's life narrative but it does offer the potential for moral and political engagement.

Oral history testimonies

This section draws on 12 oral history interviews (six women and six men) with Indigenous people who experienced child removal and confinement in children's homes that were given as part of the Bringing Them Home Oral History Project and are accessible as transcripts and recordings via the website of the National Library of Australia. Along with literary and cinematic portrayals such as *Follow the Rabbit Proof Fence* and *Rabbit Proof Fence*, such testimonies contribute to the cultural memory of the Stolen Generations, although they reach far fewer people than books and films (Kennedy, 2004; Molloy, 2015). Kennedy (2004: 48) argues that 'personal testimony has played a vital role in educating [non-Indigenous] Australians about the history and experiences of the Stolen Generations' and she has used such testimonies with students in the classroom. She emphasises that they are not just sources of history; they are social utterances which 'intervene in a present social context' (p 48).

In particular, this section examines how the testimonies collected as part of the Project reveal the ways the various institutions to which Indigenous children were removed were (and were not) experienced and remembered as spaces of confinement. In particular, it highlights the resonance of Goffman's ([1961] 2007) concept of the total institution in such testimonies. This was not the sole focus of the interviews, which also explored many other aspects of individuals' lives, but is relevant to the discussion here. The testimonies highlight how, despite many commonalities, there was no uniform or universal experience of living and surviving in these institutions. Table 2.1 at the end of this chapter gives the interviewees' biographical details. Interviewees are quoted under their real names as the testimonies have been archived for public access, with their permission.

The nature of the daily regimes of the different homes is an important theme to emerge from the interviews. Syd Graham described the lack of heating at Kent Boys Home in Adelaide, rising at 6.30 or 7 in the morning and having his bed checked. Several interviewees recalled eating porridge with weevils in it and Eileen Stevens remembered rules against talking or laughing at meal times. Herb Simms stated of Kinchela Boys Home, New South Wales: 'it was regimental, it was an institution and at the time in 1935, the manager at the time [*sic*] was somebody who was a dictatorial person'. Such testimonies provide clear echoes of the 'total institution', which places a barrier between the inmate and wider world (Goffman, [1961] 2007). This is illustrated by the children's subjection to regulation and regimentation, and to other characteristics of the total institution such as the contaminative exposure of eating porridge containing weevils. Goffman describes such experiences as an invasion of the barrier between the individual and their environment.

The most damaging aspect of this institutionalisation was highlighted by Sylvia Neary as the lack of personal contact, which was exemplified by the fact that, as Harold Harrison stated, 'everyone was only a number'. Marjorie Woodrow explained: 'We weren't never called out like, Marjorie, come to the front. I think my number was 106 or 107. 107 step forward'. Her number was displayed on her clothes. Eileen Stevens recounted being called by a number at Burnside Orphanage in New South Wales, where 'you were spoken at just like an object'. She described Burnside as 'dehumanising' and, directly invoking Goffman ([1961] 2007), an experience of 'total institutionalisation'. Keiran Michael described living in Palm Island Boys' Home, Queensland as entailing isolation from the community. He identified 'trouble with time' as one of the lasting effects of growing up in an institution, in which 'you lose all track of time, plus you never, you know, celebrated birthdays or anything like that'. Allan Mansell articulated the experience of being left alone in hallways and treated as an adult while still only a child as one of 'mental violence' equivalent to brainwashing. Testimony reveals how institutionalisation was an assault on the imaginary domain and children's sense of a unique personality.

The mission of a total institution is to transform the identities of the individuals within it (Goffman, [1961] 2007; McCorkel, 1998). The children's homes for Indigenous children in early to mid 20th-century Australia were clearly designed to do this, with their mission to 'civilise' their residents and to enable their assimilation into white settler society. Preventing children from using languages other than English, calling them by numbers rather than names and attempting to stop meaningful association with one another can all be interpreted as consistent with this. Alice Adams, who was removed to Bomaderry Aboriginal Children's Home and later sent to Cootamundra Aboriginal Girls' Home, both in New South Wales, explained that as a child she did not know that she was Aboriginal, she thought of herself as white. The homes can be regarded as 'forcing houses' for identity change – to accomplish the erasure of Indigenous identities, cultures and practices (Goffman, [1961] 2007: 12). Brainwashing or psychic coercion occurs when an institution has 'high levels of surveillance, limited opportunities for private interaction, and random episodes of "terror"' (McCorkel, 1998: 230).

Memories of punishment and control were prevalent in the testimonies. Wetting the bed meant laundering the sheets at night or having to take a cold shower as humiliation. Harold Harrison attributed his bed wetting to being 'frightened of things' in Kinchela. Interviewees recalled the frequent use of physical punishments such as the strap, the cane and hitting with a broom handle. Keiran Michael explained, 'everybody was flogged, hey. So that was part and parcel of being in a boys' home'. The explicitly punitive aspects of the homes' regimes demonstrate how they were not simply 'disciplinary' spaces; they were also spaces of violence and fear.

Not all of the interviewees interpreted the homes as coercive environments and several drew distinctions between the homes and orphanages that they lived in as very young children, and the places to which they were sent at around the ages of eight or nine. Herb Simms, who was very critical of Kinchela Boys Home, stated that the staff at Bomaderry Home 'did a good job'. Alice Adams 'loved this home [Bomaderry]. Everybody was kind. They showed us a lot of love'. She also recalled a sense of freedom, exercised through walks in the bush, picnics and trips to the beach. Eileen Stevens remembered Bomaderry as surrounded by lots of wildflowers and pansies. It was a place in which there was no need to rebel as there were no bullies and she felt safe there. Marie Hart had fond memories of the home in which she lived as a child. Sister Kate's Children's Home was in beautiful 'Bush land, orange groves, fruit groves everywhere'. There was 'a great big cottage, see, and you lived as a family'.

These memories show how lived experiences of children's homes, and the regimes within them, were diverse and did not all bear the characteristics of total institutionalisation. They could be remembered as safe and beautiful spaces – childhood homes existing in memory as eulogised space (Bachelard, 1994). This underscores the fragmented and convoluted histories of particular institutions as sites of polysemic and contested memory, rather than solely as standing for mistreatment and trauma (de Certeau, 1985; Bailly, 1993). Such memories of home, rather than only of institutionalisation, show the importance of memories of security, love and freedom to sustaining the imaginary domain as a psychic sanctuary.

Valerie Linow was trained for domestic service at Cootamundra Girls' Home. Sent to work on a farm aged 15, she was sexually abused and raped. She subsequently spent three years in Parramatta Girls' Home, New South Wales, which was 'like a gaol. But to me I was free'. She stated it 'didn't worry me if I was in gaol' because it was run by women and she felt safe. In Valerie's testimony, safety and freedom are relative and highly attenuated. It highlights how for the Stolen Generations, violent mistreatment in white settler society extended beyond institutionalised spaces of confinement and that institutions could be spaces of refuge from such violence, underlining their convoluted histories. Valerie's experiences resonate with Branch's (2005) analysis of imprisonment in colonial Kenya; whether confined or not, Africans were living under a colonial rule that was punitive and controlling.

Interviewees employed metaphors and similes of prison to encapsulate the experience of confinement in children's homes, illustrating the resemblances between different confining sites in terms of the practices employed but also the meanings those confined assigned to them (Jefferson, 2014). Describing the treatment of children in such homes as 'pretty callous', Syd Graham explained 'that's why I say from one gaol to another gaol' to articulate his experiences of being transferred between several different institutions. Keiran Michael referred to himself as a 'prisoner' at Palm Island Boys' Home, 'scrubbing, working, locked up'. Allan Mansell was in homes between the ages of eight and 16. He stated of this length of time, 'People don't get life for that'. He was made a ward of the state after his mother became ill with tuberculosis, which was 'like um, yeah, being put into prison for something you didn't know about'. George Bloomfield recounted having to march through the town of Mittagong, New South Wales in a straight line, commenting, 'Now, we couldn't understand why they did that because we weren't actually delinquents, we were state wards'. Interviewees' testimonies emphasised the emotional and existential impacts of confinement; of being made to feel like a prisoner even though the reasons for their institutionalisation were supposedly welfare based.

Comparisons between homes and 'prison camps' and 'war camps' were also made. George Bloomfield referred to the routine at Werrington Park, New South Wales as 'military style stuff', creating 'a mini army for kids'. Interviewees illustrated the close interconnection between technologies of 'protection', discipline and punishment, which could share similar regimes and forms of treatment. Ultimately, though, child removal to homes constituted something different from the experience of prison and military-based regimes. Allan Mansell stated, 'sometimes I reflect how the Jews were treated, and sometimes I think it's pretty close. Except we didn't have the kilns, that's all. Genocide they call it, I think'.

Conclusion

These different sources of cultural memory of child removal and the Stolen Generations, all of them based on the experiences and stories of individuals who lived through removal, highlight the significance of children's homes as spaces of confinement that exemplified colonial geographies of domination. This raises important questions about the difference between spaces of confinement employed to advance colonialist aims and other types of confinement. As Branch (2005) argues, the referent for colonial confinement is not a disciplinary society of surveillance and self-regulation, but the domination and control of entire ethnic and racial communities – and in relation to the Stolen Generations, the attempted erasure of these communities. Spatial practices of racial segregation employed in 19th- and 20th-century Australia, such as concentrating Indigenous people in fringe camps and on reserves, stations and missions, were in themselves forms of confinement, separation and removal (Hogg, 2001; Byrne, 2003). Such reserves and missions administered penal regimes that were outside of the existing formal criminal justice system, but also parallel with it (Cunneen and Tauri, 2016).

The oral history testimonies in particular reveal how the different institutions to which Indigenous children were removed were not all remembered as being the same in terms of the experience of daily life and in their meanings and emotional impact. However, they also trenchantly make clear the deep significance of confinement and its existential similarity with living the identity of prisoner. This was an attack on the imaginary domain – the possibility for freedom of personality and a psychic space of sanctuary. These individual histories articulate the micro level of colonial domination enacted through spatial control. Their intervention as social utterances in the present is one in which Indigenous people in Australia remain socially, economically and politically marginalised and disproportionately incarcerated in the criminal justice system (Cunneen and Tauri, 2016). As Kennedy (2004) argues, the sources that form the cultural memory of child removal can be a means for non-Indigenous people to recognise their complicity in these ongoing inequalities and the privileges that they derive from the legacies of colonial domination. Individuals may or may not take up the invitation but the sources examined in this chapter make this politics of feeling and radical democratic imaginary possible.

Table 2.1: Oral history interviewees' biographical details

Interviewee	Year of birth	Place of birth	Date of interview	Interviewer
Syd Graham	1947	Wallaroo, South Australia	4 September 2000	Karen George
Herb Simms	1926	Sydney	7 April 2001	John Maynard
Valerie Linow	1941	Sydney	1 September 2000	Diana Rich
Alice Adams	1940	Collarenebri, New South Wales	30 March 1999	Colleen Brown
George Bloomfield	1956	Melbourne	7 April 2001	John Maynard
Eileen Stevens	1935	Pallamallawa, New South Wales	13 and 15 May 2000	Steven Guth
Sylvia Neary	1940	Darwin	16 March 2001	Jane Watson
Harold Harrison	1943	Cummeragunja Mission Station, New South Wales	11 January 2000	Rob Willis
Marjorie Woodrow	1923	Menindee, New South Wales	29 September 1999	Colleen Hattersley
Marie Hart	1932	Carrolup Reserve, Western Australia	22 October 2001	Lily Bhavna Kauler
Allan Mansell	1957	Hobart, Tasmania	9 August 2001	Lyn McLeavy
Keiran Michael	1951	Cairns	17 September 1999	Phillip Connors

Relevant organisations

ANTaR: https://antar.org.au/

National Congress of Australia's First Peoples: https://nationalcongress. com.au/

3

Historical Spaces of Confinement 2: Magdalene Laundries

This is the second chapter on imagining historical spaces of confinement. We adopt the same approach as the previous one in drawing on cultural representations and oral history interviews as feeling forms, in this case to examine the imagination of Magdalene laundries in post-independence Ireland. As with residential schools in Australia, we explore the significance of memory and cultural memory to this imagination. We continue to employ Goffman's ([1961] 2007) concept of the total institution, mindful of its influence on cultural representations and as a way to make sense of the subjective experience of institutionalisation. As confining institutions that were specifically for women and girls, Magdalene laundries regulated and punished gendered transgressions of normative femininity, in particular the transgression of imagined Irish womanhood. Through physical separation from mainstream society, and the cultural and institutional imposition of shame, women and girls in laundries were rendered socially abject.

Magdalene laundries as confining institutions

Magdalene laundries in post-independence Ireland were sites of 'coercive confinement' for young women perceived and judged to be immoral (O'Sullivan and O'Donnell, 2012). Established in the 18th and 19th centuries as institutions of rescue and reform for women who worked as prostitutes, they became a constituent part of the deepening religion-based disciplinary regime of the post-1922 Irish state. They became more punitive once they were run by Catholic religious orders (McCormick, 2005; Crowley and Kitchin, 2008). The laundries were spaces of confinement for girls and young women who had become pregnant outside of marriage and/or had given birth to illegitimate babies – or who were considered to 'pose the risk of [sexual] temptation' (Pine, 2011: 36). A small percentage of women and girls were committed to laundries following a conviction for infanticide, or were placed there as a condition of probation or following release from prison (see Black, 2018), 'but the majority were placed by families as a result of sexual transgressions' (O'Sullivan and O'Donnell, 2007: 37–8). There were also admissions from industrial schools, reformatories and mother and baby homes. Confinement as 'inmates' or 'penitents' in these institutions was indefinite as there was no specified sentence or mandated release (Smith, 2007; Fischer, 2016). There was also little or no state regulation. Around a thousand women were held in 10 Magdalene laundries by the 1950s and the last such institution did not close until 1996 (O'Sullivan and O'Donnell, 2007).

Magdalene laundries were run according to work-based regimes, with inmates spending their days doing unpaid labour. This exemplified the governing religious ideology of disciplining body and soul through work to absolve inmates' sins, but also meant that laundries were part of a profit-making operation (Simpson et al, 2014). They were not subject to the Factory and Workshop Act 1895, which protected certain rights for workers, including some specific regulations for women (Crowley and Kitchin, 2008). Simpson et al (2014) classify Magdalene laundries as total institutions as they had involuntary membership and were based on confinement and control. Markers of inmates' individual identities were removed through wearing uniforms and having their names changed. The McAleese Report 2013 found that the Irish state was culpable in the coerced labour of more than 10,000 women and girls confined in laundries post 1922. Taoiseach Enda Kenny made an apology on behalf of the state to survivors of the laundries shortly after the report's publication (Simpson et al, 2014; Till and Kearns, 2016). The Magdalene Laundries Restorative Justice Ex-Gratia Scheme established a programme for monetary redress for survivors, which opened in June 2013 (see Winter, 2017).

Crowley and Kitchin (2008) contextualise the use of Magdalene laundries to regulate Irish women's sexuality in relation to moral geographies of sexual conduct. Following independence in 1922, the state developed powers to intervene in the lives of its citizens according to Catholic moral values. The Constitution of 1937 exhibited a 'very circumscribed view of women's role in society' and entrenched the family as central to Irish society and the national imaginary (Crowley and Kitchin, 2008). Women's citizenship was redefined in terms of their roles as wives and mothers, and their formal rights in relation to paid work and civic responsibility were curtailed (Beaumont, 1997). Crowley and Kitchin (2008: 358) describe these gendered shifts as 'thoroughly spatial', producing moral geographies in the home, workplace and public space. A network of institutions constituting Irelands' 'architecture of confinement', of which Magdalene laundries were one example, developed to regulate and reform 'deviants' (Smith, 2007).

O'Sullivan and O'Donnell (2007) delineate a carceral archipelago of industrial schools, reformatories, prisons, Magdalene homes, workhouses and mental hospitals in mid 20th-century Ireland that were 'repositories for the difficult, deviant and disengaged' and were regularly utilised by families as a means of lightening the economic burden of supporting certain family members. They calculate that in 1951, 1% of the Irish population was coercively confined in this network of institutions, which was largely run by religious and voluntary agencies, with high levels of confinement for women and girls. This underlines the necessity of analysing confinement beyond the criminal justice system to fully understand social control. While rates of imprisonment for women were low, rates of confinement in other types of institution were high.

Fischer (2016: 821) argues that in Ireland 'women's virtue bec[a]me entangled in ideas of nationhood and national identity'. As a newly independent state, Ireland sought to differentiate Irish identity from British identity in relation to themes of purity, chastity and virtue. Membership of the imagined community for Irish women was as guardians of sexual virtue and as symbols of home and nation. Against this, the bodies of young women and girls were problematic as potentially sexually disruptive. The mobilisation of shame in relation to sexually deviant women and girls was a significant disciplinary device, leading to their institutionalisation and social abjection. Such individuals shamed not only their families, but also the nation, requiring their physical separation and concealment. This actual and imagined separation reinforced the boundaries of Irish national identity against transgressive internal others. It exemplifies the role of abjection in legitimising the 'prevailing order of power' (Tyler, 2013: 20).

Cultural representation and cultural memory of the Magdalene laundries includes documentaries, films, plays, memoirs and oral history testimonies. This chapter analyses the documentary *Witness: Sex in a Cold Climate* (Channel 4, 1998), the films *The Magdalene Sisters* (Mullan, 2002) and *Philomena* (Frears, 2013) and seven oral history interviews from the Magdalene Institutions: Recording an Archival and Oral History project, the transcripts of which are available online. Cultural portrayals and oral histories are especially significant in relation to Magdalene laundries as the religious orders that ran them have either been unwilling to make their records accessible or have done so very selectively (Yeager and Culleton, 2016). The history and meaning making of these institutions is derived from sources of cultural memory, which have recovered the laundries from political amnesia (Smith, 2007).

Witness: Sex in a Cold Climate (Channel 4, 1998)

The process of recovering memories of the experiences of women confined in Magdalene laundries began in the 1990s following the discovery of an unmarked grave of 133 women at High Park Convent in Dublin (Yeager and Culleton, 2016).[1] Documentaries such as *Witness: Sex in a Cold Climate* were based on interviews with women who were survivors of these institutions and brought their testimonies of lived experience to public attention in Ireland, the United Kingdom and the United States (Smith, 2007). In this case, the documentary focuses on four women's stories and contextualises them in relation to the power of the Catholic Church in Ireland, which occupied the position of being 'always right'.

The role of the laundries in the concealment of girls and young women who were the bearers of shame is strongly emphasised. Interviewee Christina Mulcahy recounts being admitted to a laundry after becoming pregnant outside of marriage in 1940. The nuns who ran it did not pass on the letters that her baby's father sent and her son was placed in an orphanage at 10 months old. Martha Cooney was sexually assaulted by her cousin on the way home from a fair aged 14. She was sent to a Magdalene laundry in Dublin and explains that this meant 'There's no talk, there's no scandal' – she was hidden away. Through voiceover, the documentary explains that laundries were usually located outside of cities and were cut off from the outside world. Their role as 'distinctive place[s] in the colonial, postcolonial and religious landscapes of Ireland' is evoked (Till and Kearns, 2016: 363). As such, it highlights the mapping of ideology onto space and place and the use of spatial separation as part of the moral geography of hegemonic control.

The nature of the typical regime is discussed by Phyllis Valentine, who entered a laundry in Galway aged 14, having been sent there from an orphanage because she was 'as pretty as a picture' and the nuns feared she would 'fall away'. She explains that her clothes were taken away and replaced with a drab, shapeless uniform and her hair had to be cut short. As a penitent she had to work washing linen for no pay to absolve her sins. She describes a 'relentless' regime of working in silence six days per week from early morning until late at night, with no recreation, just prayer. Phyllis outlines the use of gestures of humiliation, such as having to kneel in front of nuns to ask forgiveness

---

[1] In 2003 it was publicly revealed that there were the remains of 155 women but no death certificates could be provided for 22 of them (Smith, 2007).

for minor misdemeanours, and also relates that physical punishments were frequently used. Christine explains that she had her hair cut off for not going to confession.

Witness: Sex in a Cold Climate brought survivor testimonies of incarceration in Magdalene laundries to public attention and opened space for communication about these experiences, their place in the recent past and their ongoing impact on survivors. *The Irish Times* reported that following the documentary's broadcast in March 1998, a dedicated helpline received hundreds of calls from those who 'poured out their anger and horror at the treatment of women in Magdalene institutions' and from those attempting to trace relatives (Donnelly, 1998). The documentary is also notable because it inspired Peter Mullan's film *The Magdalene Sisters* (2002), which draws on and fictionalises the experiences of the four women interviewed (Smith, 2007; Wilmer, 2016).

The Magdalene Sisters (Mullan, 2002)

Like *Rabbit Proof Fence*, *The Magdalene Sisters* brought the issue of human rights abuses related to institutional confinement to the attention of national and international audiences. The film won the Golden Lion Award at the Venice International Film Festival. It also received criticism from Italian Catholic newspapers for being unnecessarily provocative and a misrepresentation of the role of the Church (O'Toole, 2003). Smith (2007) argues that Irish viewers were confronted with a story which they knew but had ignored; the film's public function was to encourage reckoning with the legacy of a traumatic history.

The Magdalene Sisters begins by establishing the circumstances that lead three different young women to be institutionalised in 1964 in ways that clearly parallel the testimonies offered in *Witness: Sex in a Cold Climate*. Margaret is raped by her cousin at a wedding and is sent away by her family. Bernadette is sent to the laundry from her orphanage after flirting with boys. Rose has had a baby outside of marriage and is forced to sign him away for adoption by her parents. The convent in which the laundry is located is depicted as a space of confinement and of labour, with women scrubbing and cleaning the halls. The three young women arrive led by nuns, who lock and unlock doors, emphasising similarities between the institution and prison. The laundry itself is full of women working hard, wearing a uniform of a dull brown dress and blue apron. The portrayal of inmates of various ages, including older women, highlights that some were confined in these institutions for many years.

The film represents the laundry as a total institution based on confinement and the curtailment of the self via a regime of prayer and work. The stern and cruel Sister Bridget explains to the three new arrivals that 'I decide when and if you're allowed to leave' and they are locked into their dormitory at night. The inmates are forbidden from speaking to one another at meal times and in the laundry. The Bernadette character highlights the similarity between the status of laundry inmate and prisoner, stating 'I've not committed any crime' and 'We're not slaves, we're not criminals'. The punitive aspects of the regime are illustrated in relation to the treatment of runaways, demonstrating the role of the institution as a place of concealment and barrier to the outside world. A young woman's father drags her into the dormitory by her hair following her attempt to return home and as a gesture of humiliation she has her head shaved by Sister Bridget. Bernadette is caught attempting escape and has her hair roughly cut, lacerating her face and scalp. The use of corporal punishments such as caning also underline the nuns' punitive treatment of the inmates.

A controversial scene depicts the quasi-sexual humiliation of the inmates, who stand naked before two nuns who compare the sizes of the young women's breasts, how hairy they are and laugh at their bodies. This is based on the testimony of Bridget Young in *Witness: Sex in a Cold Climate*, who describes how the nuns who ran the orphanage in which she lived in Limerick 'used to make us strip naked for them' and laughed at and criticised their bodies. This scene has been challenged as a misrepresentation of the past as it conflates the treatment of women and children, and stripping naked is unlikely to have happened in a laundry (Smith, 2007; Pine, 2011). It serves a dual function in the film: it highlights the institution as a space of cruelty and draws on tropes familiar from prison films, particularly the hinted-at repressed lesbian sexuality of an all-women setting.

In an article for *The Observer*, O'Toole (2003) describes *The Magdalene Sisters* as 'in some respects, an old-fashioned Hollywood movie' that belongs in the familiar genre of the prison drama. This, he argues, 'limits its originality' but makes it watchable and accessible. The prison guard role in *The Magdalene Sisters* is fulfilled by the nuns and they are depicted as suitably cruel and abusive, with Sister Bridget in particular played as an irredeemable villain. The nuns' portrayal has been criticised as one-sided and one-dimensional, particularly as their feelings and motivations are not explored (McCormick, 2005; Smith,

2007). Sister Bridget's only moment of humanity is when she expresses her lifelong love of films before screening *The Bells of Saint Mary's* for the inmates on Christmas day.

The stereotyping of the nuns means that *The Magdalene Sisters* does engage in a certain amount of moral simplification by offering clear 'baddies'. However, it portrays the laundries as ultimately resulting from and benefiting a patriarchal society. Women's role in the control of other women is made clear but it is men who are shown to be dominant in their positions as fathers and priests. The nuns have power over the laundry's inmates but they are themselves also confined in the convent. The abusive behaviour of men in a heavily patriarchal society is also highlighted through the actions of a priest, Father Fitzroy, who sexually abuses Crispina, a young woman with learning disabilities. The abuse is unintentionally exposed by Margaret, who puts poison ivy in his vestments. This very publicly affects both Father Fitzroy and Crispina during a recreation day, resulting in Crispina's removal to a mental institution, where she is even more heavily incarcerated.

Although there were objections to the negative portrayal of Catholicism on the film's release, and there have been some analyses which argue it scapegoats the Church while ignoring the role of the public (McCormick, 2005), *The Magdalene Sisters* situates the characters' confinement in relation to wider social structures and mores. The opening scenes clearly implicate the families of Margaret and Rose in their institutionalisation. After four years in the laundry, Margaret is released when her brother comes to collect her. She wryly comments, 'Can you believe it's that simple?' underlining the complicity of male family members.

In keeping with the prison drama formula, the film culminates in the escape of the two remaining young women, Bernadette and Rose, and their entry into late-1960s Irish society. McCormick (2005) castigates the film for representing the inmates as victims but it does portray several instances of the young women's resistance with Bernadette and Rose ultimately triumphing over the regime by challenging it head on. Bernadette throttles Sister Bridget until she gives up the key to the front gate and then scares away the nuns who chase after them by threatening them with a lamp stand. She and Rose escape to freedom across the fields. This gives *The Magdalene Sisters* a Hollywood-style ending, which is not necessarily very realistic but offers the audience an affective 'moment of catharsis' (Pine, 2011: 48). (It reflects how Christina Mulcahy, interviewed for *Witness: Sex in a Cold Climate*, escaped from her institution to Northern Ireland to work as a nurse – albeit without the dramatic confrontation with nuns).

For Pine (2011), the film's ending limits its effectiveness as it is possible to experience this catharsis and move on, consigning the experiences of women confined in laundries to a vanished past, which contrasts with the modernity of 21st-century Ireland. However, Smith (2007) contends that in bringing these women's experiences to public attention, *The Magdalene Sisters* illuminates the obligation for contemporary Irish society to recompense the survivors of the laundries. Scarleta (2014: 246) interprets the film's closing epilogues, accompanied by freeze frames of the four main characters, as undercutting the exhilaration of Bernadette and Rose's escape and trapping them 'in the decade that saw their incarceration'. She commends the film for refusing to celebrate the 1960s as 'Ireland's turning point as a modern nation' and argues that this enables it to avoid depicting women's sexual oppression as something which belongs to the past and not the present (p 242).

Philomena (Frears, 2013)

Philomena is adapted from *The Lost Child of Philomena Lee*, former *Guardian* journalist and political spin doctor Martin Sixsmith's (2009) book about attempting to help Philomena Lee find her son, who was adopted by an American family aged three. Philomena spent four years in a Magdalene laundry in a convent in Tipperary in the 1950s after becoming pregnant outside of marriage. She subsequently moved to England, became a nurse and had a family. In 2002 she told her other two adult children about her lost son Anthony and resolved to find him. They were able to discover his post-adoption identity as Michael Hess, that he had been a senior official in the Reagan and Bush administrations and that he had died in 1995. He had visited the convent in Tipperary two years before his death – which was also where he was buried. However, the convent informed them that they had no further details about his past. Philomena's daughter Jane was able to contact Martin Sixsmith via a friend and he helped them to find out more about Michael's family background in the United States. They also found that the convent did in fact have the contact details of Pete, Michael's partner, who had made a donation for Michael's burial plot. The film changes the chronology of some of the events and fictionalises others, particularly in relation to the point at which Martin Sixsmith became involved with Philomena's quest, which it depicts as being from the beginning of her search.

Through the story of Philomena's attempts to come to terms with her past, the film grapples with the Magdalene laundries as memory but also as exerting influence on lives in the present. Philomena keenly feels the loss of her son, which she largely kept secret for 50 years. The convent's refusal to help her find about Anthony/Michael underlines the unwillingness of the religious orders to make their records public and, by association, to help to recompense for the laundries. It also illustrates the ongoing power of the Catholic Church to avoid accountability for its role in running them. Whereas *The Magdalene Sisters* contributes to cultural memory by portraying the 1960s for a 21st-century audience, *Philomena* draws a direct line between what happened to its protagonist in the 1950s and her life in the present. She is not presented as a victim – through references to her professional life as a nurse and the portrayal of her relationship with her daughter, it is clear that her life has been fulfilling. However, the sadness of losing her son has persisted and the legacy of shame and secrecy has also influenced her adult life. The film begins with Philomena worshipping in church and remembering meeting a boy at a fairground, who kisses her. She did not know about sex or how pregnancy occurred, her mother having died during her childhood. The birth of Anthony and her time in the laundry are depicted through flashback. Despite having a breech birth, the nuns did not allow her any pain medication as the punishment for the shame of her situation was not to be mitigated.

Themes of complicity and shame are central to the film's interpretation of Philomena's past. When she meets Martin for the first time, she informs him 'My father just left me with the nuns. He was so ashamed, he told everybody I was dead'. She later explains the internalisation of shame and a stigmatised identity in relation to why she willingly signed a contract pledging never to try to find Anthony, 'I believed I had committed a terrible sin and needed to be punished'. Further use of flashback shows the dormitory in the asylum, with its large windows and beds in a row. Young Philomena works in the laundry clad in a shift dress and apron. She is allowed to see Anthony in the nursery for one supervised hour per day until he is taken away for adoption. Philomena watches from behind the metal bars of the convent's gate as he is driven away down the long gravel drive.

Present-day Philomena explains to Martin that for her, leaving the asylum was not an option; she needed to pay 100 pounds in order to do so and even if she had had the money, she had nowhere to go. The film demonstrates how confinement, particularly where it is closely interwoven with welfare, is not always a case of being legally denied freedom. Rather, the strictures of a patriarchal society and of limited financial resources can be just as powerful in terms of keeping people confined. The film combines realist-style depictions of Philomena's past with odd-couple comedy and *bildungsroman* as she and Martin travel to Ireland and the United States on the trail of Anthony. Unlike *The Magdalene Sisters*, *Philomena* depicts the laundries' international links – they were a source of babies and toddlers who could be adopted by Catholic American families in exchange for donations. It highlights how complicity with young Irish women's confinement extended beyond Ireland.

After returning from America, Philomena and Martin go to the convent in County Tipperary and sit in its grand drawing room to drink tea with the nuns. The convent's large staircase and dark atmosphere convey what an imposing space it is even though it no longer confines Magdalenes. As Philomena walks around the courtyard, she remembers Anthony being driven away and encounters a graveyard for mothers and babies in the building's gardens. The film's altering of the 'real' chronology means that this functions as an ironic moment as Philomena does not yet know that her son is buried right there and must return later after her trip to America. This scene also recalls the scandal of the sale of High Park in Dublin in 1993, when the discovery of the unmarked graves of women and children sparked the cultural remembering of and political reckoning with Magdalene laundries in Ireland.

The end of the film finds Philomena and Martin back in the convent's drawing room having learned that Antony/Michael had visited the nuns and been told that Philomena had abandoned him. It fictionalises a meeting between Philomena, Martin and Sister Hildegaard (who in fact died before Philomena began looking for her son). Through the articulation of her now outmoded beliefs in sexual self-denial, this scene represents Sister Hildegaard as being as damaged by the convent as Philomena, if not more so, as she has been prevented from experiencing sexual relationships and therefore proper fulfilment. In this, it takes a similar approach to mitigating the nuns' villainy as *The Magdalene Sisters*, by portraying them as victims of patriarchal sexual repression. Philomena's unwillingness to condemn the nuns, and her belief in their good motivations and her friendship as a young woman with Sister Annunciata, also helps to provide a somewhat nuanced picture of their role. Whether being a nun offered a valuable role and identity for women in its own right, beyond the ability to wield circumscribed power over other women as part of patriarchal bargaining (Kandiyoti, 1988), is not addressed by either film. Both films contain the subtext that a substantial part of women's fulfilment and entry into subjectivity is achieved through heteronormative sexual relationships (albeit not constrained by marriage), reinscribing some of the patriarchal constructions they seek to refute.

In highlighting the continued secrecy and – as portrayed – dishonesty of the religious orders, *Philomena* makes a strong point about the perpetuation of trauma in the present. The laundries do not belong to the past because not only are thousands of survivors and their children still living with their legacy, the religious orders' refusal to make their records available means that they continue to do harm. A substantial part of this history remains untold and secrecy prevents accountability. *Philomena* connects past with present more unambiguously than *The Magdalene Sisters*, particularly in relation to the continuing institutionalised power of the Catholic Church and the need to reject what the film portrays as the damaging and repressive belief in sin. Released in 2013, the context for its reception was different from that of *The Magdalene Sisters*. The Magdalene laundries have become more firmly entrenched in national and international cultural memory as an example of religious and gendered repression.

Oral history testimonies

This section draws on oral history testimonies collected as part of the project Magdalene Institutions: Recording an Archival and Oral History, the transcripts of which are available online. Testimony was gathered from survivors, relatives, religious sisters who worked in the laundries and other key informants. The project sought to 'contribute towards a better understanding of the Magdalene Laundry system' and aimed for the testimony and other documents to be widely available to the public and to inform educational programmes, art work and public policy (Magdalene Oral History Project, no date). Here, we draw on seven interviews with survivors out of the 13 available at time of writing. Table 3.1 at the end of the chapter provides interviewees' biographical details and their pseudonyms assigned as part of the project. Yeager and Culleton (2016) argue that survivor histories are both a way to understand the meaning of what happened in the laundries and also provide an historical record. Oral history projects have an important public function as 'resistance against collective forgetting' (p 140).

The testimonies reveal the diverse reasons that girls and young women were sent to laundries, their welfare-based role and the interrelationships between different institutions of confinement in Ireland. Out of the seven women, only Bernadette was sent to a laundry by her family because of having a baby outside of marriage.

Mary, who spent two and a half years in Gloucester Street Magdalene Asylum in Limerick and had previously been in an industrial school, was sent there by her mother, who disliked Mary's boyfriend (O'Donnell et al, 2013a). Lucy and Evelyn were both sexually abused by male family members and were placed in laundries after coming to the attention of social services and the police (O'Donnell et al, 2013b; 2013c). Mary C was taken from her mother and sent to an industrial school in County Wexford before later going into Good Shepherd Magdalene asylum (O'Donnell et al, 2013e). Pippa grew up in an orphanage in County Galway. After leaving at age 16, she 'couldn't get used to the outside world and that' and was sent to a laundry in Limerick (O'Donnell et al, 2013g). Chrissie simply did not know why she was sent to a laundry in Waterford (O'Donnell et al, 2013f). These women's biographies clearly demonstrate how Ireland's architecture of confinement was employed for the purposes of welfare and moral regulation and was perpetuated through the relationships between the Church, agencies of the state and women's families (Smith, 2007).

Lucy describes how the work-based regime in Sean McDermott Street laundry in Dublin entailed rising at 6.30 to clean the house before breakfast. Laundry was for four days per week, with one given to education (O'Donnell et al, 2013b). Evelyn worked five days per week in High Park; her days began at 8 o'clock with Mass and work consisted of ironing baby clothes. Talking with other girls was not allowed and there was no education available (O'Donnell et al, 2013c). Bernadette recalled working five and a half days a week for no pay, with Sunday reserved for prayer. The routine was conducted in silence, forming friendships was discouraged and there was no education. She packed baskets of clean linen for hotels and acknowledged that this was 'a preferred job because it was so nice and clear and easy' and that she was likely given this role because of her middle class background (O'Donnell et al, 2013d). Pippa explained that a consequence of living in the asylum was 'I still think at times I'm timed to do this and timed to do that, that's still with me' (O'Donnell et al, 2013g).

The curtailment of self, characteristic of total institutionalisation, was enacted through changing inmates' names and requiring them to wear a uniform. Mary C recounted how on entering the laundry she was given the new name of Imelda and had her hair cut into a pudding bowl style (O'Donnell et al, 2013e). Pippa, Mary and Evelyn were all assigned new names (O'Donnell et al, 2013g; 2013a; 2013c). Mary described her laundry uniform as 'brown like, a blouse and a skirt' and Bernadette explained that she was able to wear her own clothes, but only had two outfits (O'Donnell et al, 2013a; 2013d).

Interviewees recalled opportunities for recreation and some leisure, illustrating the convoluted histories of the laundries and the possibility for them to bear multiple meanings (de Certeau, 1985). Certain events that took place or spaces within the institutions could be remembered fondly, even though they were also sites of trauma. Mary C was a member of the laundry's choir and performed operettas for the public; she was also able to read a lot of books (O'Donnell et al, 2013e). There was a television in the 'lovely' sitting room of Lucy's institution and there were evenings when psychology and social work students would visit to sing and play guitars (O'Donnell et al, 2013b). Mary could walk around the convent's garden and remembered some music and dancing (O'Donnell et al, 2013a). Evelyn could take trips into the centre of Dublin on Saturdays (O'Donnell et al, 2013c). Such recreational activities can be understood as 'institutional ceremonies' that allow a certain amount of 'role release' for staff and inmates and where there can be some sociability between them. Activities that involve visitors and other outsiders can give an 'appropriate' and favourable image of the institution to those on the outside (Goffman, [1961] 2007). In this case, they underline how the laundries were part of Irish society and of the national imaginary, despite the young women's spatial separation, and highlight how abject groups are essential to dominant imaginaries.

The interviewees evoked the ways in which laundries were spaces of confinement. Pippa described the prison-like high walls of the convent in Limerick and the 'big bars on the windows' (O'Donnell et al, 2013g). Evelyn and Mary recalled how doors and windows were kept locked (O'Donnell et al, 2013c; 2013a). Lucy's first impression of Sean McDermott Street was 'all the steel, or the bars on the windows' and Mary described the dormitories in which the inmates slept as 'like … like prison they weren't cells, it was a big dormitory' (O'Donnell et al, 2013b; 2013a). Her memories illustrate the significance of different spaces within the institution as evoking different feelings. High walls around the convent meant 'you were completely secluded' but she also recalled the 'lovely avenue' leading up to the building (O'Donnell et al, 2013a). Lucy described both the convent's 'horrible corridor' and its contrasting big grounds and garden (O'Donnell et al, 2013b). The space of the laundry itself was conjured up by Evelyn: rolling machines at the front, pressing machines to the left, large tables with irons in the middle and big washing machines at the back (O'Donnell et al, 2013c). Pippa remembered 'No air, there was no air in the laundry' (O'Donnell et al, 2013g).

Physical confinement was a barrier to interaction with the outside world, as were the limited opportunities to receive visits. The role dispossession entailed in being separated from friends and family and forcibly breaking with one's past is a key element of total institutionalisation (Goffman, [1961] 2007). In her five years in the Good Shepherd laundry in Waterford, Chrissie was visited just once when her sister was over from America (O'Donnell et al, 2013f). Lack of contact with relatives or the outside world meant that 'they managed to brainwash you' according to Mary (O'Donnell et al, 2013a). Evelyn was visited by some of her relatives at first but the visits stopped, she presumed at the instigation of her father (O'Donnell et al, 2013c). For Pippa, isolation was the worst aspect of institutionalisation. She spent two and a half years in a laundry in the late 1960s but recalled old women who had lived there since childhood (O'Donnell et al, 2013g). Mary explained that the worst thing was '[j]ust being locked away' (O'Donnell et al, 2013a).

Punishment and humiliation were constituent aspects of the regime in different institutions. Interviewees recalled the use of corporal punishments. Lucy explained that pausing work in the laundry in order to talk resulted in being struck across the legs with a thin stick (O'Donnell et al, 2013b). Evelyn stated 'a belt or a big cane, that's how we were punished' and related an occasion when she was grabbed by her hair and dragged to the Mother Superior's office. However, the use of gestures of humiliation was more strongly evoked (O'Donnell et al, 2013c). Bernadette stated: 'There was no physical punishment. There was a lot of psychological punishment.' This entailed being put down by the nuns. It was necessary to do what they said as 'they had all the power and I had none' (O'Donnell et al, 2013d). Mary refused to kiss the floor in front of the nuns but stated that others did. She was made to sit on a penance table as a consequence (O'Donnell et al, 2013a). Mary C's time in industrial school was harder than the laundry as there were more beatings, but being in a Magdalene asylum was degrading. She ran away from the Good Shepherd laundry in County Wexford and was returned by the police; for this she had her hair cut with shears. She recalled the inmates as 'very humiliated by the nuns', with the best way to cope being not to answer back (O'Donnell et al, 2013e). Goffman ([1961] 2007) argues this restriction on expressive behaviour weakens the autonomy of the institutionalised. Bernadette highlighted '[n]ot being able to make a single decision for yourself' as one of the worst aspects of the laundry (O'Donnell et al, 2013d).

Like the interviewees in the Bringing Them Home Oral History Project discussed in the previous chapter, the women used metaphors of imprisonment to give meaning to their confinement. Mary C asserted that the laundries were 'prisons really you know. They were … we were a source of cheap labour for them [religious orders], you know' (O'Donnell et al. 2013e). Lucy 'thought [she] was going to prison' when she was put in Sean McDermott Street convent at around the age of 14 (O'Donnell et al, 2013b). The sense of being punished without having committed a crime was a strong one. Mary commented, 'It was almost like you were sent to prison for something you never did' (O'Donnell et al, 2013a). Evelyn also addressed this theme, stating that the laundry was 'worse than prison' but also articulated its profoundly gendered nature. She explained that the nuns in High Park knew that she and other girls had been placed there because of being sexually abused by male relatives, reflecting '[a]nd that's why we were dirty', exemplifying the disgust inherent in social abjection. Women were always blamed for provoking sexual abuse, 'not the men' and she concluded 'I was in there being punished for nothing' (O'Donnell et al, 2013c). Pippa explained 'the Magdalene Laundry … was just … it was punishment, just pure punishment for something I never had done in my life'. She was placed in an orphanage at 18 months old because her mother was unmarried, and interpreted her confinement in institutions as punishment for this (O'Donnell et al, 2013g).

Bernadette 'didn't find the laundries that difficult to deal with' because she had attended boarding school as a teenager. Her family was not religious but sent her to a Mother and Baby Home in Belfast 'to protect my … my brothers and sisters from the … the shame, of the scandal' and 'then the laundry to punish me'. The experience of boarding school was similar to prison, but at least she knew when it would end. At the laundry, '[t]here was no end to our incarceration'. Leaving was not possible as she had no money. Bernadette reflected, 'I was totally … we all were … totally … handcuffed' (O'Donnell et al, 2013d). Mary C articulated her abiding fear while confined in the laundry as 'will I ever, ever get out of here?' (O'Donnell et al, 2013e).

Although interviewees employed the metaphor of prison, the lack of a sentence or clear reason for their institutionalisation in laundries highlights how their confinement was different from prison. Mary's comment that the religious orders were 'like the Taliban of today' evoked the moral, regulatory purpose of the laundries (O'Donnell et al, 2013a). Evelyn and Bernadette's testimonies demonstrate the significance of blame and shame in relation to young women's 'troublesome' sexuality and the impact of being designated as transgressive and abject (O'Donnell et al, 2013c; 2013d). Mary concluded that 'they took your freedom, they just … they took your identity' (O'Donnell et al, 2013a) illustrating how the experience of confinement in a Magdalene laundry entailed mortification of the self (Goffman, [1961] 2007) and severely restricted the imaginary domain that enables freedom of personality.

Conclusion

The collection of sources analysed in this chapter shows the development of a national and international cultural memory of Irish Magdalene laundries since the 1990s. Documentaries such as *Witness: Sex in a Cold Climate* brought women's testimonies of their experiences into popular consciousness, and the feature films *The Magdalene Sisters* and *Philomena* have dramatised these sites of confinement, raising themes of complicity, patriarchal domination and the connections between past and present. Oral history testimonies communicate the experience of confinement in laundries as one of total institutionalisation, as well as starkly illustrating the impact of the gendered politics of shame at an individual, micro level.

Individual experiences can be related to the macro level of the boundaries of the imagined community, and the significance of gendered and sexual respectability to the exercise of full citizenship. The gendered social control of the Magdalene laundries illustrates Yuval-Davis and Stoetzler's (2002) point that rules specific to women highlight their ambivalent status as members of the nation. They are at once symbolic of the collectivity's honour but also marginalised 'in public, political and military spheres' (p 340). Women embody borders and boundaries – but also represent the possibility of transcending them. This is the possibility for resistance that Tyler (2013) recognises in social abjection.

Taken together, the sources under discussion are feeling forms that help to challenge ideological structures and their effects (O'Neill, 2001). Continuing restrictions placed on the laundries' archival records emphasise the importance of imagination and cultural memory in coming to terms with this history and in contributing to a politics of feeling that has motivated action and shaped a radical democratic imaginary. Cultural memory has been vital to advocacy movements for survivors and to gaining acknowledgement of the role of the state and forms of redress. The struggle for adequate restorative justice remains unfinished and the confirmation of the existence of a mass grave of babies and children in 2017 on the site of the Bon Secours Mother and Baby Home in Tuam, County Galway demonstrates how the traumatic history of Ireland's moral geography of confinement is still in the process of being recovered (Grierson, 2017).

Table 3.1: Oral history interviewees' biographical details

Interviewee	Year of Birth	Place of Birth	Laundry/ies	Date of Interview	Interviewer
Mary	1945	Dublin	Our Lady of Charity of Refuge Magdalene Laundry, Gloucester Street, Dublin; Good Shepherd Magdalene Laundry, Limerick	5 January 2013	Sinead Pembroke
Lucy	1961	Dublin	Sisters of our Lady of Charity Laundry, Sean McDermott Street, Dublin	23 March 2013	Sinead Pembroke
Evelyn	1952	Dublin	Sisters of Our Lady of Charity Laundry, High Park, Dublin	2 March 2013	Sinead Pembroke
Bernadette	1944	Not stated for confidentiality	Not stated for confidentiality	11 February 2013	Sinead Pembroke
Mary C	1945	Enniscorthy, County Wexford	Good Shepherd Magdalene Laundry, New Ross, County Wexford	23 February 2013	Sinead Pembroke
Chrissie	1950	Dublin	Good Shepherd Magdalene Laundry, Waterford	9 August 2013	Claire McGettrick
Pippa	1950	County Galway	Good Shepherd Magdalene Laundry, Limerick	7 August 2013	Claire McGettrick

Relevant organisations

Justice for Magdalenes Research: http://jfmresearch.com/

4

Creative Writing and the Imagined Spaces of Imprisonment

Continuing the focus on confinement, this chapter explores findings from two different creative writing projects with male prisoners in HMP Durham and HMP Lewes. Both of these, in different ways, drew on archival sources as inspiration for forms of creative writing – ghost stories in the case of Durham and poems in the case of Lewes – and involved collaborating with writers. Both prisons are category B institutions, meaning that they are closed and have people awaiting trial and/or sentencing, as well as sentenced prisoners who are judged not to need maximum security conditions but must be confined. We present imaginative criminology based on creative, participatory methods that engaged participants' personal biographies through their fictional and poetic work. This is the first of three chapters that also draws on arts-based walking methods. In presenting examples from participants' writing in the forms of poems and stories, we analyse them *as* creative writing, rather than simply as exercises of rehabilitative programming. In particular, the writing conveys the significance of the sustaining role of memory and openness to the future, as well as the multiple boundaries between the inside and the outside.

The spaces of imprisonment

Incarceration in prison is fundamentally based on spatial tactics. Prisoners experience both the enforced fixity of incarceration in a secure institution and forced mobility between institutions at the behest of others (Martin and Mitchelson, 2009). Carceral geography examines what prisons reveal about the production of space, the role this plays in enabling forms of state control based on confinement but also the agency of the confined in challenging the associated assaults on their identity (Martin and Mitchelson, 2009; Jewkes, 2013; Moran, 2015). For nearly all prisoners in the UK, prison is not a 'terminal destination' but rather for a certain period. Confinement to a particular space as punishment is spatial and temporal. Drawing on Dodgshon (2008), Moran (2012) conceptualises this as 'time-space': the interdependency of space and time. The length of a sentence is externally controlled but also experienced personally and variably. For example, younger prisoners may feel like they are suspended in time and are consequently oriented to the future and release. Older prisoners may be more conscious of the physical changes wrought to their bodies as they age inside (Medlicott, 1999).

Along with separation through spatial incarceration, loss of time is central to imprisonment as punishment (Hardt, 1997). Our sense of time is interrelated with our sense of self; this is 'thrown into crisis' when entering prison, which can inspire what Medlicott (1999: 216) describes as 'painful nostalgia' for the outside. The time-space of prison is imbricated with 'memories and mediated experiences of the outside' (Wahidin and Tate, 2005: 65). The past can also be a protective resource – a source of memories enabling imaginative escape, or useful experiences to draw on – and the anticipated future can be sustaining during incarceration (Brown, 2003). This relates to the imaginary domain, the psychic space that provides the self with sanctuary.

Carceral geography has sought to combat the hiddenness of imprisonment (Martin and Mitchelson, 2009), addressing how it 'shapes prisoners' thoughts and feelings about their past and their future, and their sense of the passage of time' (Moran, 2012: 310). It also highlights that although prisoners are hidden from view, prisons are not completely cut off from social life. Certain spaces, such as the visiting room, allow some porousness between the inside and the outside (Moran, 2013). Depending on their security classification, prisoners are not necessarily confined for the whole day but may undertake employment or voluntary work on the outside during their sentence.

Some areas of the prison are less 'prison like' than others. For example, the prison library is seen as an important service in processes of reform and rehabilitation but it is also a space in time where prisoners can connect with the outside world via newspapers, and where they can experience a sense of community and belonging facilitated by the spatial setting: the shelves of books, conversation with the prison librarian and other users, as well as in reading groups. At HMPs Lewes and Durham the libraries look and feel like libraries do on the outside. They are calm, quiet, in-between spaces that connect users to their memories of using libraries and the sensory dimensions of school or community libraries. In itself, reading enables engagement with imaginative space and is a form of transcendence from the here and now. The ban on sending books to prison initiated by the then Secretary of State for Justice Chris Grayling MP in 2014 was fiercely resisted by writers and poets, reformers, such as the Howard League, researchers and the general public. Eventually declared unlawful by Justice Collins in the High Court, the overwhelming message was that 'reading is a right not a privilege' (Travis, 2014).

The book ban was intended to remind society and prisoners that prison entails 'an extreme sense of difference and isolation from society' (Brown, 2009: 3), underlining prisoners' social abjection. Brown (p 4) highlights that penal images and popular discourses of punishment abound in the wider culture 'in spaces far from the social realities and social facts that define mass incarceration'. To this end, she explores how ordinary citizens imagine imprisonment through cultural forms such as film, television and news. In the previous two chapters we extended this approach to other sites of confinement, namely residential schools and Magdalene laundries. Here, we explore how writing by prisoners can inform how confinement in prison is imagined and understood. Prisoners both experience and imagine incarceration, and creative writing is a key means through which to articulate this. Prisoners' writing challenges the hiddenness of the prison and their isolation from society, as well as offering perspectives informed by the experience of incarceration rather than the more distanced portrayals examined by Brown (2009). It also renders these imaginatively and expressively.

Creative writing in prison

Creative writing with prisoners can enable self-expression and critical reflection (Clements, 2004), which can help them to confront their law-breaking behaviour (Johnson, 2008). Opportunities to participate in arts-based activities in prison are known to have a positive impact on prisoner well-being through enhancing confidence, personal autonomy and self efficacy, and increasing self-respect (McNeill et al, 2011; Cox and Gelsthorpe, 2012; Bilby et al, 2013). This can help to facilitate desistance – the process by which people who have offended stop offending (Cheliotis and Jordanoska, 2016). Creative writing helps to cultivate the inner resources that support rehabilitation and is also a means to improve prisoners' literacy more successfully than a 'basic skills' approach (Clements, 2004).

While not wishing to diminish the importance of such benefits, we argue that prisoners' imaginative writing also offers an important lens through which to view both the experience of imprisonment, the boundaries between the inside of prison and the outside of 'freedom', individual biography and emotional subjectivity. As such, it should be comprehended as writing that sheds light on complexity and not simply as a means to reduce offending. Creative writing by prisoners has value whether it encourages desistance or not. And as Cursley and Maruna (2015) argue, projects that do not seek to 'fix' their participants in terms of thinking style or personality but instead focus on creative expression can be more successful in bringing about personal transformation.

The methodological approach in both projects discussed in this chapter was influenced by participatory arts-based research (PA), which seeks to engage with the complexities of lived experience in the context of social structures and processes (O'Neill, 2012). The aim of PA is to provide opportunities for groups to represent themselves, rather than being spoken for, and to critically recover their experiences – often with the aid of personal, folk and archival materials (O'Neill, 2010). PA enables the representation of multiple subjectivities and the foregrounding of 'feelings, meanings, emotions, and experiences from multiple standpoints' (O'Neill, 2010: 231). Designed to access subjugated perspectives (Leavy, 2009) and to deepen knowledge and analysis of marginalised groups that are frequently studied (O'Neill, 2012), PA is particularly relevant to researching the experiences of prisoners. Experiencing PA can be transformative, enabling participants' self-representation (O'Neill, 2012). In turn, these representations can be employed to combat stigmatising and dehumanising portrayals of prisoners. Focusing attention on the micrology of lived experience – the minutiae, the small scale – the work we draw on here can help us reach a better criminological understanding of the lives of prisoners through their embeddedness in structures, the impact of culture and possibilities for agency in relational and democratic ways.

Writing Lives: voices of prisoners in HMP Lewes

Writing Lives was a project developed by colleagues Lizzie Seal, Tamsin Hinton-Smith and Bethan Stevens at the University of Sussex from the Sociology, Education and English departments respectively in partnership with the Mass Observation Archive (MOA), the regional library service, HMP Lewes and an independent creative writing consultant. It used materials from the MOA to inspire creative writing by prisoners, which was intended to help facilitate self-expression. Asking participants to respond to archival texts can elicit rich discussion, reflection and interpretation. Such materials are powerful prompts of memory and creativity, which otherwise might be difficult to access (Bagndi, 2009).

The MOA specialises in material about everyday life in Britain. Mass Observation was founded as a social research organisation in 1937 to 'give voice to the values expressed in the private lives of ordinary people' (Hinton, 2010: 2). Following a hiatus from the mid 1960s, it was relaunched in 1981. It has a panel of volunteer writers who respond to 'directives' on different topics, ranging from shopping strategies to the London Olympics. These can be described as open-ended questionnaires although in practice panel members can respond to the various questions or write something inspired by the topic but not constrained by the questions. As such, the directives are examples of life writing. The archive also holds diaries kept by panel members during the Second World War, and annual 'day diaries' that record their authors' lives on 12 May. The kinds of autobiographical writing collected by Mass Observation are inevitably evocations of memory but as a non-institutional archive the MOA is also a repository of 'popular' collective memory (Breakell, 2008).

The researchers selected extracts from Mass Observation's directives on 'time', 'belonging' and 'letters', all of which are topics from the post-1981 phase (2010, 1988 and 2004 respectively), and several Second World War diaries. Sessions were based around these, whereby the workshop leader shared evocative extracts as prompts for related free-writing exercises. For example, on the theme 'time': 'I have often thought about time. Who first decided that night and day should be divided up into units? Did one man say to another "I'll put a mark on this candle and when it has burned down to the mark I will come and see you". I wonder who decided on the size of the candle and how it was divided up' (Female respondent, Summer 1988, MOA/ Dir.2618.5.881). The related exercise was to write about an occasion in one's life when time was significant. This inspired participant Steven to write 'I remember when my dad died. I was 13 and took time off school to see him at the Sussex County Hospital. It was Friday and when I got home, he died at 5.30pm.' The free-writing served as the basis for developing poems.

The workshops were held in HMP Lewes in summer 2014. Prisoners signed up for them voluntarily and they were publicised beforehand via posters in the library. Workshops were attended by a core group of eight to ten men and were three hours long. Numbers fluctuated slightly due to the exigencies of prison life, meaning that some men could only attend one or two workshops because, for example, they were discharged from prison or required to attend alternative activities. The only knowledge that the researchers had of prisoners was what they chose to disclose about their personal lives. Information including age, sentence length, educational and occupational background was not sought and was often not known. Pseudonyms are used below to protect participant anonymity. The creative writing exercises were led by the independent creative writing consultant and the researchers participated in the workshops alongside the prisoners (for further reflection on this, see Hinton-Smith and Seal, 2018).

Analysing prisoners' poems

In an essay reflecting on (American) poetry written in the era of mass incarceration, Soto (2017) argues that 'narratives in poetry by incarcerated people often examine the space between themselves and the outside world, serving as a bridge between the two populations'. To fully understand imprisonment it is necessary to explore writing by those who have experienced it and can make its 'secret world' visible (Franklin, 2008: 235). Prison is a place of punishment but also the prisoners' home; they are alive to its mundane details (Rowe, 2004). Prisoners' writing bears witness to the pains of incarceration and the losses that it entails, and is also a means for them to deal with the environmental assault of the prison (Johnson, 2012). Poetry can express the affective dimensions of imprisonment, which helps to emphasise the shared humanity of those on the inside and the outside (Johnson and Chernoff, 2002; Clemente et al, 2011). In addition to experiences of imprisonment, the poems are also about their authors' lives before prison, and their hopes for life afterwards (Rowe, 2004).

The felt gulf between the inside and the outside emerges very strongly from the poems written as part of Writing Lives, especially in relation to being cut off from family (Wahidin and Tate, 2005). Matt wrote 'I hate prison, make me sad/Miss family' and that 'My family are love me all time/To see me every week/Only one travel one hour's train'. Mark's poem *Governed by Time* also highlights separation from family through its anticipation of seeing his children again: 'But I'm looking forward to the time/Where I'm back with my kids/To share all those memories'.

Prison as a space of isolation is a crucial theme. *Governed by Time* describes prison as 'this isolated place' and *Reflection* by Henry relates 'Looking through the bars/I see the world passing by/And I feel cut off, isolated'. The emotional impact of incarceration, and its painful nostalgia (Medlicott, 1999), is evoked by Daniel in *From May to July*. His thrill in May at being placed in a cell with a window that opens 'Enough to see the sky/Over the buildings' dissipates as it becomes 'A slit to remind me/Of what I miss'. By July: 'I don't look out of the window any more/It hurts too much with the memories/How will I feel in a month/A year/2 years?'

This emotional impact is wrought by time-space and the realisation of the pain of missing life as it goes on outside (Hardt, 1997; Medlicott, 1999; Wahidin and Tate, 2005). *Governed by Time* articulates the existential experience of time-space: 'You're governed by time in this place/And you have time to reflect on things/Which you wish you maybe had time/To change or put right'. *Comparison*, another one of Mark's poems, also expresses this:

> I compare my life in here
> To winter
> There is no warmth anywhere
> There are too many storms

Being in prison 'Feels like winter showers' and 'The isolation of being inside/Feels like those dark winter nights'.

Peter's poem *Distances* encapsulates how the time-space of incarceration, in which 'The world seems so far away', is what constitutes the pain of punishment: 'The distance is the punishment/The things, the people/The life we miss/We long to see again'. *Distances* communicates the subjective experience of incarceration and its deep affective impact

The time-space of prison is also shaped by the prisoners' relationships with their family and friends on the outside, and their memories of home. Using extracts from the MOA is especially relevant in relation to the interweaving of memory and autobiography found in the poems, which articulate both painful and joyous memories. Losing home and family are important themes representing harrowing experiences. Ezra's *Letter to My Mum* states, 'I'm writing to let you know I find it hard to forgive you in regards to putting me in care from the age of 14' and questions 'can a mum really love a child she does that to?'. Daniel conveys the trauma of separation from an abusive home in *Belonging*: 'I remember leaving home/My head bloodied/My jaw broken/My nose bleeding'. This left him adrift 'Looking around/In all four directions' unable to return to 'The last family/I really belonged to'. The poem evinces a strong sense of family as offering mooring to a particular place, even if that is not a place of safety. In *Leaving*, Nathan reflects more hopefully on ending his relationship with the mother of his children: 'I'm sorry for that but I felt we/were going round in circles as you never had time for me/or the boys, but now time has gone, you have become/a great mum and I wish you happiness for the near future'.

The irreparable loss of death is evoked in some of the poems. Bert's *Letter to my Father: Hi Dad* explains 'there's not a day that goes by when I don't think about you, like at my last football game, and how much respect I had for you but never told you'. David's *Letter About My Brothers* concerns the four brothers he lost as a child:

> And I didn't know who they are
> I will miss them
> And would like to visit the graves
> And I'll always think of them

David explained in the workshop that his brothers were buried in Ireland and he had never been able to go to their graves.

The significance of memories of loss of family and home highlights the porousness of the space of prison and its interconnections with the outside world. Moran (2013) examines this in relation to prison visiting rooms where prisoners have face-to-face encounters with people from the outside. She argues that in this sense prisons are not total institutions, although as the previous chapter discussed in relation to Magdalene laundries, Goffman's ([1961] 2007) concept of the total institution incorporates attention to interaction between inmates and visitors and other outsiders.

Memory is another agent of this porousness; prisoners are incarcerated but their former lives and selves live with them (Hardt, 1997; Rowe, 2004). The loss or absence of love and sanctuary are unsurprisingly strong themes in the poems. Memories of joy and freedom are also significant and further illustrate the porousness of the prison walls to the outside in prisoners' imaginations, and how the past can be a protective resource (Brown, 2003). Ezra expressed 'a pot of joy' and 'the best of memories' as all he required in *Box of Belonging*. Roy's *Deep Heart's Core* recalls the beautiful landscape of a happy holiday, 'Gold sands – and azure blue water/It was heaven on earth'. Watching the sea was to be 'lost in awe'. *A Day* by Sean evokes the freedom of getting his first car: 'I used to love going fast/Round roundabouts/It seemed that I was invincible/And nobody could catch me'. The carefree freedom of Sean's poem, in particular, creates a stark contrast with incarceration – and a means to escape it through connecting with the imaginary domain, if only briefly.

The promise of the future as different and better from the present is an important theme in the poems and demonstrates imagining the future as helping to sustain a sense of self (Brown, 2003). *Belongings* by Nathan states: 'The most belonging/I would take with me/Is my family/And my future', with 'everything else' being left behind. The future orientation of young prisoners is clearly articulated in *Workbook* by Ezra, as is the slowness of prison time:

> Soon I will remember the 9th of January 2015
> A nice morning, I predict
> It will be based on the fact
> That one would have spent 2 years in custody;
> When you are a young man of 23
> That's like a lifetime

He looks forward to the chapters of the book of his time in custody becoming 'A distant memory/You could call it a soon-to-be/Forgotten story'. *Workbook* addresses the flow of time, with the time spent in prison and the day of Ezra's release envisaged as future memories. The poem highlights the relational aspect of time as it notes how two years is 'like a lifetime' to a 23-year-old. In *Governed by Time*, Mark reflects:

> My time here is a waste
> But I'm looking forward to the time
> Where I'm back with my kids
> To share all those memories
> Which will always be with you

Prison becoming a memory and the creation of new, different memories in the future demonstrates the deep significance for prisoners of temporality as non-linear and as therefore offering hope through imagining 'the fullness of life' outside (Hardt, 1997: 66).

Ghosts of the future: HMP Durham

'Ghosts of our future' was a project funded in 2014 by the Arts Council UK and HMP Durham. The project was led by writer in residence Sheila Mulhern, who, following a conversation in the prison library, reflected on the lack of privacy, the pressure on resources, the stress and boredom experienced by prisoners and asked: where are the spaces that they can process their demons? HMP Durham was built in 1819, next to the medieval Tithe Barn, which is now a museum. In preparing for the grant application, Mulhern said that

> 'the ghost story seemed to allow people to talk freely and safely. It broke down barriers and got prisoners and staff

talking and laughing. When people told their stories, reliving handed-down tales, remembering unexplained events, it seemed to intrigue and ground them. It was decided we would write a book of ghost stories.'[1]

Supported by HMP Durham, a bid was submitted to the Arts Council to fund a series of workshops culminating in an anthology of ghost stories and a ghost walk, working in partnership with academic researchers Maggie O'Neill and Ivan Hill, at the time at Durham University. The project was made up of two parallel writing groups, one inside and one outside, who worked alongside the project team, authors, artists and a photographer to create ghost stories and a ghost walk, inspired by HMP Durham and the history of Durham city from medieval times to the current day.

The ghost walk mapped the history of crime, punishment and justice in Durham city, working together with the prison library, Durham University Library and archivists, and through ethnographic walks in the city. The knowledge and history shared by members of the public was also enfolded into the walk. In search of a debtors' prison, once situated in what is now the indoor market, O'Neill and Hill visited a hairdressers and tattooists located inside the market. They were told by a client of the hairdresser and the tattooist something of the history of the debtors' prison; and the tattooist showed them a door leading to underground tunnels that are said to connect the debtors' prison with the Gaol and the lower house of correction. These traces of the past well illustrate the convoluted history of the city and the ways in which the sites of the present are haunted by the ghosts of the past (de Certeau, 1985).

During the development of the walk, O'Neill and Hill sought to get in touch with the history, landmarks and places of crime, justice and punishment in sensory and corporeal ways. An example of 'micrology', walking is a very helpful method of attuning a person or group to a place and conducting a critical recovery of histories of crime, justice and punishment in the present. In criminological research walking is not just what we do to get from a to b but integral to our perception of an environment and a powerful way of communicating about experiences and ways of knowing across cultural divides, time and history. Walking in the city focused attention on the sensory, kinaesthetic and mobile dimensions of lived experience, the traces of history in the present, in the architecture, landmarks both existing and which have disappeared. Walking also focuses our attention on

---

[1] From personal communication with Mulhern, September 2014.

the relationship between the visual and other senses and enables multi-sensory experience and relational ways of knowing (Edensor, 2010; Myers, 2010; Pink et al, 2010; O'Neill and Hubbard, 2010; O'Neill and Perivolaris, 2016).

The walk in Durham begins at Jimmy Allen's nightclub, formerly the Bridewell or lower house of correction, and winds its way to the marketplace, the library, the County Gaol, Palace Green, the Courthouse, the Dun Cow pub, North East Prison After Care service, HMP Durham and ends at the Tithe Barn Museum and Prison Officers' Club. In the course of the walk we ask, how do some things get defined as crime and not others? What are the causes of crime and what is prison for? The main themes emerging from the walk associated with the histories of crime, justice and punishment include: the importance of education and prison education; prison reform; the roles provided by the Church, the state and landowners such as Lord Londonderry, whose statue is situated in the marketplace area; the relationship between crime, justice and poverty; and some historical narratives about the executioners Calcraft and Marwood, who entertained guests in the Dun Cow before and after hangings. The walk was shared with the inside group in the workshops through the history, stories and landmarks. They could not join us on the walk itself. The creative writing by both groups is informed by the walk and can be found on the project website.[2]

Figure 4.1: Durham Crime Walk

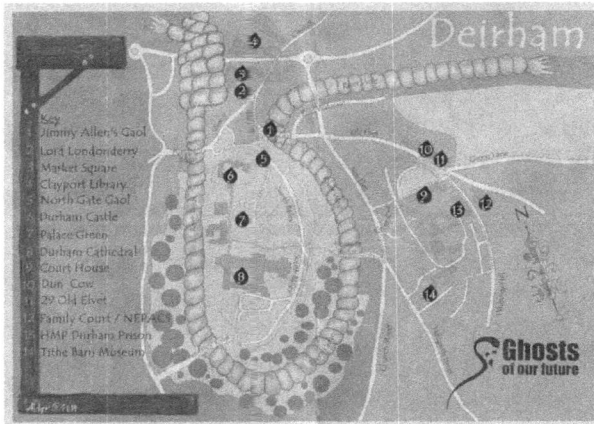

Image artist: Mark Alder

[2] http://ghostsofourfuture.com.

Eleven people participated in the inside group, aged from their early 20s to late 60s. The group met in the prison library on one morning a week 'to tell ghost stories and eat biscuits' and 'gradually, very individual stories began to emerge' and were written and shared. Singer and poet Kate Tempest was invited to perform and talk to the group, funded by English PEN, and two artists, Mark Alder and Dick Ward, introduced and taught drawing; this work was eventually displayed as part of an exhibition that toured prison and public libraries. As Mulhern (2015: ix) describes, 'there was the odd snag; workshops were interrupted or cancelled, participants were waylaid, shipped out or released and paperwork occasionally went into a black hole but we've had solid support and the group has continued with guest speakers and events'. A young man – a lifer keen on ghost stories – and a librarian collated and reviewed a reading list that Durham County Council sourced and donated. English PEN also funded workshops in nearby prison Frankland. A book of the work was created and published by the team (Mulhern, 2015).

Earlier in the chapter we suggested that creative, imaginative writing and also reading has certain benefits for prisoners. Reading, writing and sharing one's stories opens a space for conversation and dialogue, for connecting with each other and with aspects of each other's biographies and life stories. It enables people 'to talk freely and safely' and it 'broke down barriers and got prisoners and staff talking and laughing', creating a space where the prisoners and officers could relate to each other in a different way than they might on the wing, or in their cells.

Space as relational, imagined and open to the future

The themes of space and time, loss, as well as crime, punishment and retribution, stasis or paralysis, and hopes for the future, or an imagined future, emerged in the ghost stories and poems. The workshops took place in the prison library, a space that was relational, that bridged or traversed time in the cells as well as the experience of being inside in relation to the outside world. We might call this 'potential space', after Winnicott (1951), or facilitating 'mental space', drawing on Robert Young's (1994) analysis of the importance of space in understanding our inner worlds and in psychoanalytic, psycho-social theorising.

These two articulations of the meaning and materiality of space, and the themes in the creative writing can also be analysed using Massey's theorising of space as relational, imagined and importantly as having or offering an 'openness to the future' (Massey, 1994: 11).

For Massey (p 12) 'space is indeed a product of relations'. She argues that 'identities/entities, the relations "between" them and the spatiality which is part of them, are all co-constitutive' (p 10). In calling for the spatialisation of social theory she tells us that 'any serious recognition of multiplicity and heterogeneity depends on a recognition of spatiality' (p 11). If space is a product of interrelations we must acknowledge multiplicity, multiple possibilities and stories/narratives. Finally, and influenced by Laclau and Mouffe (1985), space is imagined by Massey as a process, a result of relationalities, not a closed system, but rather is open to the future.

This openness to the future is the radical democratic promise of the imagination – a radical democratic imaginary (Smith, 1998; O'Neill and Seal, 2012). Influenced by Cornell (1998; 2006: 31) and Smith (1998) we describe the imaginary domain as a moral and psychic space that is necessary in order to open and keep open and rework repressed elements of the imaginary. It is crucial, in our work as cultural and critical criminologists to open and keep open space for democratic discourse and 'knowledges of resistance' (Walters, 2003). We argued that participatory and arts-based methodologies can enlighten, raise awareness, 'uncover hidden histories' and 'produce critical reflective texts that may help to mobilise social change' (O'Neill and Seal, 2012: 8).

Another way of thinking about space in the prison setting and in the creative writing workshops is through Young's (1994) concept of 'mental space'. Mental space is defined by Young as a space for reflecting, feeling, for relating to others, being open to experience; it is also the space of and for art and imagination. He describes the in-between or 'intermediate' space that is afforded by reading, listening to music, or being in a theatre as mental space; 'there is a merging, a congruence, a suspension of boundaries' (p 143). Influenced by Winnicott, the space between subjective and objective reality is an 'intermediate area of experiencing, to which inner reality and external life both contribute' (Winnicott, 1951: 230, cited in Young, 1994: 146). This is for Winnicott what we can call culture but it also exists as 'resting place for the individual engaged in the perpetual human task of keeping inner and outer reality, separate yet inter-related' (Winnicott, 1951: 230).

Creating space for imaginative writing facilitates the possibility of and for 'mental space', for working through the experience of imprisonment, the bounded nature of prison life, the isolation of being in prison and locked in a cell for long periods of time. Importantly, it is the work that goes into defending the self from risk, the risks afforded by being in prison and the energy needed to protect the 'self' and create the sanctuary of the imaginary domain. Similar to the analyses of the poetic work in the previous section, the creative writing served 'as a bridge' to help process emotions and feelings as well as behaviours and deeds, and indeed to reflect on certain relationships or relationalities. The writing process also helped the 'writers' to work through the past (and present) in the imaginative space created through the workshops and library facilitated by the creative writing workshop leader.

This can be illustrated through discussion of the ghost stories written in the workshops. In *Suitable Victims* two ghosts are trapped in a circular story of murder that is also a story of never ending crime. The relationship between the here (ghostly time) and there (real time, the 'out there' sense of the world) is bridged by Mark Taylor the estate agent (also a ghost) murdered by the protagonist who is locked in a constant circular repetition of bringing victims to the house – the 'house of horrors'. In this story the writer pokes fun at a middle class couple viewing the house and their attachments to certain objects: the Aga, the fireplace, the art deco interiors of the house. There is in this story no way out; the place in which the story is set is a haunted house, there is no opening to the future, just paralysis, stasis and repetition of the crime.

Similarly in *Blood at Shimba Hills* the protagonist, his wife Seema and Mangara their cook visit a game reserve south of Mombasa, where the ghost story is set. There is no sense of the vast open countryside of the reserve for the action takes place in a tent. Haunted by a 19-year-old Masai herdsman, who, in saving a family from a lion attack, was savaged and killed by the lion in the very same tent, the protagonist flees the next day with his wife and servant. However, leaving is impossible; the ghost of the herdsman follows and is spotted by the protagonist through the rear view mirror, seated in the Jeep next to the servant. The vehicle crashes into a mango tree and he finds himself back in the tent with no idea what will happen next. The reader is left with a sense that his fate is sealed, he is alone it seems, no mention of the wife or cook – maybe he has become the ghost.

In *There and Not There* these themes of enclosure, being constrained, trapped, alone, and fearful/scared are also present, but here there is also a stronger focus on relationships and the relational dimensions of life as well as an openness to the future. The protagonist Bobby is on a train speeding from Kings Cross to Sunderland having left Aldershot Barracks after a period of service in Sierra Leone. He picks up a 'spooky booklet' on the train and starts to read about Mary Ann, who 100 years earlier had drowned herself in the village pond, having been thrown out by her stepmother and having waited in vain for her fiancé to return and say she could stay with his family. The ghost story is interwoven with Bobby's feelings and anxieties about returning home to his wife and child, of service in Sierra Leone and the inevitable stories he will be expected to tell as a returning soldier. Returning to his wife and child after a night with an old friend, he walks through the park and summons the ghost of Mary Ann, who follows him home and wakes everyone with her crying throughout the night. In this story Bobby exorcises the ghost by returning to the village pond and on meeting the ghost falls over in fear and tells her 'I'm not him! I'm not him! I'm not your boyfriend who left you … You're dead, a ghost.'

The ghostly figure of Mary Ann returns to the pond and is submerged in the water. Bobby then researches the story and finds a picture of Mary Ann that is exactly the image of the ghost he had met. The experience makes him question life, death and the possibility of an afterlife. 'What about killing? Would there be judgement?' He decides to leave the army. 'A civilian now, he is determined to be good and live righteous so, when the time comes for him to become a ghost, he makes heaven and not hell.'

All three stories explore 'the space between themselves and the outside world, serving as a bridge between the two populations'. The stories help the writers to say the unsayable, to mediate the experiences of being inside, in a place of punishment; but as we argued in the preceding section, prison is also their home and the stories are a means of processing the everyday realities of prison life, the affective, relational, embodied, the imagined as well as the 'hoped for'.

At the launch of the crime walk in Durham, the mother of one of the prison writers from the inside group joined in along with the team and members of the outside writing group. She read his poem before the groups headed off on the walk and spoke of her immense pride in her son. We reproduce it in its entirety overleaf. Here the focus on space is clear – the 'big darkness', marked by 'unnecessary distances', the earth just a 'pebble' and there will be no comfort, spinning 'through stellar eternity in God's silence' becoming a 'White sarcophagus hieroglyphiced' and left ultimately 'to die up there'. Imaginative writing here deals starkly with the paralysis and isolation of being in prison by imagining and taking the readers/audience to the in-between or third space both creatively through the writing but also in the experiential, affective messages of the poem. This for us is an example of the possibilities of and for 'micrology' and the radical democratic imaginary.

To An Astronaught
You're going to die up there.
In the Big Darkness, with
Pin-wheeling galaxies that
Can only glare at each other
Over unnecessary distances.
You're going to die.
The pebble earth won't
Bother to hug your body
In orbit, won't allow you
To burn up gloriously. Your
Goldfish suit will gently
Spin you through
Stellar eternity in God's
Silence.
Un-weathered in the vacuum
You will become an
Unseen exhibit in an unending museum, a
White sarcophagus hieroglyphiced
N.A.S.A. hiding you
From the increasingly distant
Ra.
You're going to die up there.

In *Transgressive Imaginations* we drew on the work of Marxist psychoanalyst and cultural theorist Lorenzer (2002) whose psychoanalytically informed cultural approach to research, the 'depth hermeneutic method', introduced tools for research such as 'scenic understanding', a process whereby researchers might reflect on their affective and embodied experience to the data they gather, or the texts gathered or developed in research. In this chapter, we have argued that prisoners' writing offers an important lens to engage with and better understand the lived experiences of imprisonment, the relationship between subjective, objective and intermediate reality and the biographical (micrology). The relationship between connecting and attuning to the individual and the collective or group, through writing and reading aloud, also opens a space for experiencing the collective, social and cultural dimensions of our lives together, our being in common – which leads to the experience of 'mattering'. This was certainly evidenced in both prison writing groups. This process and the mental or intermediate space that is created might also uncover and allow us to explore what is excluded from everyday prison life as 'micropolitics'; creative writing and reading in prison has enormous benefits for a restorative justice approach in prisons. The self-representation, and as we have seen in this chapter, the critical recovery of feelings, emotions, stories through the ghost story or poetic form can be immensely transformative for the individuals and the groups. This is through being able to write about and share representation of subjectivities, feelings and emotions, which it may simply not be possible or safe to do on the wing. In turn this challenges stigmatising representations of prisoners and their social abjection. It enables them to speak of and share, for some, transformative or utopian possibilities. We have analysed the threefold dimension of space though prisoners' creative writing: the relational, the imagined and, for some, an openness to the future, to future possibilities. The spaces created by the workshops and by the projects can also be examined in spatial ways, as creating physical, material spaces but also in the 'mental space' fostered through the arts-based methods in both projects and prisons – as a radical democratic imaginary.

Relevant organisations

English PEN: https://www.englishpen.org/outreach/prisoners-young-offenders/

National Criminal Justice Arts Alliance: https://www.artsincriminaljustice.org.uk/

5

Border Spaces and Places:
the Age of the Camps

Continuing the focus on space and place in imaginative criminology, this chapter discusses arts-based research (film and walking ethnographies) with asylum seekers and migrants waiting in border spaces, mostly in camps (in Greece, Syria and Melilla). The construction of the camp as a temporal, liminal, spatial site of containment and constraint, and a border space, and what this means in the lives of the people and families waiting, some for many years, is examined through narrative interviews, photographs and filmic work.

In this chapter we continue the themes discussed in previous chapters, including the relationship of space and time; liminal in-between spaces; and the usefulness of a threefold analysis of space through the relational, embodied and imagined experiences of migrants. We also develop our analysis of border spaces and places and the impact on the lives of people on the move and crossing borders, through micrology of their lived experience. As we argued in Chapter 1, focusing on micrology (the minutiae, the small scale) of lived experience can often help to shed light on and deconstruct broader structures (and discourses) that are not only the outcome but the medium of social action and meaning making. Walking methods are a particularly relevant, helpful and potentially groundbreaking way of studying borders, and the relational, embodied and imagined (O'Neill and Hubbard, 2010) experiences involved in physically crossing borders, going into areas perceived as 'risky' or, literally, walking the border. Borders can also be internalised and walking is a powerful route to understand the lived experiences of others as well as eliciting rich phenomenological material as an imaginative criminological method.

The concept and analysis of 'mental space' is helpful here too (see Chapter 4), connecting with Massey's (2005) notion of space as imagined as 'open to the future'. In an increasingly interconnected world, Massey argues that space is the result of interrelations and interactions; it is the sphere of the multiple existence of possibilities, of 'coexisting heterogeneity' and is always 'under construction' (p 9). In articulating a deeper analysis and understanding of 'space' in social theory Massey (p 13) is also concerned with a 'politics that can respond' to this. When discussing globalisation she reflects on the way that it is often described and imagined as 'unbounded free space' and rather like 'free trade' – yet the opposite is the truth and research on the increasing focus on borders and 'border studies' illustrates this. A key theme in this book is the possibilities of and for a radical democratic imaginary, through cultural criminological research that pays attention to micrology of lived experience and analyses the significance of space, place and micropolitical transgressions. In this chapter we focus on the lived experiences of migrants and asylum seekers in relation to borders.

Borders

We live, say Diener and Hagan (2012: 1), 'in a very bordered world' and 'the bounding of space' is an 'essential component of human activity for millennia'. We are crucially aware of borders in relation to international disputes, the sovereignty of nation states, migration and trade routes, alongside borders as defining political space; for example in the demarcation of the European Union and the reorganisation of that space as a consequence of UK exit. Borders define and design space and place on more micro levels too. For example, the prison is spatialised, into cells, wings, eating areas, working areas, the library; for different and specific purposes, to monitor and control movement, to support everyday activities and ultimately to restrict and contain. In fact our social, economic, cultural and political lives and society are organised through time and space, place, territory and the meanings we attach to spaces and places. We come to understand our shifting/ contingent identities in relation to place, space, time and belonging. Borders are also 'manifestations of power in a world marked by significant spatial differences in wealth, rights, mobility, and standards of living' (Diener and Hagen, 2012: 121) as experienced in the so-called 'refugee crisis' in the Mediterranean.

Borders, borderlands and increasing mobility/migration are a defining feature of the 20th and 21st centuries. A significant amount of research shows that most migration takes place either within countries or between developing countries (O'Neill, 2010) and the costs of border control measures are high in both human and financial terms (Marfleet, 2006; Castles, 2003; Smith, 2006). Yet in a world of constant movement, of glocalisation, global mobility, migration and what Castles (2003) calls the asylum–migration nexus, an enormous amount of energy, time and money is spent on securing the borders of western states, on erecting stronger and stronger barriers to entry. Bauman (2001: 74) writes about this process as an aspect of 'liquid modernity': the vision of a just society characterised in early modernity has given way to a 'human rights rule/standard/measurement' and a more 'liquid' version of modernity that perpetuates the production of difference and ultimately leads to 'intense community building-in, digging trenches ... barring intruders from entry, but also insiders from getting out; in short, in a keen control over entry and exit visas' (p 76). At the same time, later modernity or liquid modernity is marked by increasing mobility (Urry, 2007).

This increasing mobility, especially with regard to the response by states to forced migration, has led to the development of entry restrictions in the North and containment measures in the South. In the United Kingdom, a significant number of asylum and immigration acts and related legislation and social policies, especially in the last 20 years, make it very difficult to gain asylum. The use of detention and containment has increased, as has the numbers of removals. The impact of government immigration and asylum policy and the ways that this is interpreted by the general public and represented in the mass media has an important bearing on the reception of asylum seekers and migrants at all levels of society. The immigration and nationality directorate was renamed the 'Border Control Agency' and Theresa May and the Conservative government have pursued an active 'hostile environment' policy to discourage 'illegal immigration'.

The construction of the asylum seeker as a deviant Other is very well documented (Marfleet, 2006; Pickering, 2005; O'Neill, 2010) as is the racialised stigma attached to the label (Tyler, 2018). Pickering (2007: 1) describes the responses of governments as illegitimate and potentially criminal in this regard. Indeed, she defines state responses to refugees in the North as embedded in law and order politics and policies that are maintained via hegemonic relations across three levels of society: civil society (identified in media representations); law enforcement (administration of the law); and domestic and international legal mechanisms (the courts and international human rights regimes). The basis of Pickering's argument is that governments in the North have used 'law and order politics in the development and implementation of refugee policy' (p 3) and this relies increasingly on 'unmitigated ideological and coercive force'. This distances western nations from their complicity in the production of the refugees and in turn provides them with 'justification for unbridled denunciation and violent rejection' (p 21). Most importantly, as Pickering points out, 'when major parties refuse to debate, or only engage in debate on peripheral issues to immigration, then space for questioning and the space for civil society to exert itself are often reduced' (p 5). Negative and racist attitudes to migrants and asylum seekers can go unchallenged and the closing down of debate simply reinforces limited and limiting attitudes in the general population. Political responses simply reinforce the protection of borders and make deviant those who seek entry as 'dangerous outsiders', who have transgressed the norms of civil society, and domestic and international legal mechanisms.

These socio-political and legal changes have led to what Kapoor (2018) calls the 'unmaking of citizens'. The ultimate experience of liminality is being within a nation or state but at the same time outwith the concept of citizenship. Situated in a risky in-between place, the risk of being 'removed' and hence 'stateless' is ever present (O'Neill, 2010; Bosworth, 2008).

Borders, negative globalisation and humiliation

The movement of people across borders is also a key defining feature of the 20th and 21st centuries (Kushner and Knox, 1999; Adelman, 1999). It is important to locate the making and unmaking of borders within the context of history and globalisation. Bauman (2004) identifies the role of modernity in the production of refugees as intrinsically linked to globalisation and colonialism (see Mayblin, 2017). For the processes of modernity and globalisation are underpinned by deep social inequalities that lead people to leave home in search of a better life through choice and/or compulsion, or literally, to flee for their lives (O'Neill, 2010). At one and the same time the concept of 'negative globalisation' captures the contrast between the selective globalisation of labour, trade, capital, surveillance and information, on the one hand, and yet on the other, 'the numbers of homeless and stateless victims of globalisation grow too fast for the planning, location and construction of camps to keep up with them' (Bauman, 2007: 37). The sovereignty of states is challenged in a globalising world: 'globalization draws the administrative-material functions of the state into increasingly volatile contexts that far exceed any one state's capacities to influence decision and outcomes' (Benhabib, 2004: 4). Yet, sovereignty is vigorously asserted, especially at national borders, which although 'porous, are still there to keep out aliens and intruders' (p 6). Globalisation is not a system of equal participation but is marked by processes of inclusion and exclusion (Castles, 2003; Bauman, 2004) and histories of colonial domination. Nation states 'still claim the foundational, constitutive prerogative of sovereignty: their right of exemption' (Bauman, 2004: 33). This right of exemption is documented by Gyollai and Amatrudo (2018: 16) using the case of Hungary erecting a 175km fence along the border with Serbia in reaction to the flow of people across its borders in the summer of 2015. They argue that Hungary is a state departing from agreed norms of behaviour in the area of migration and refugee policy and we need to draw attention to this. It is a transgressive act (transgressing supranational migration and refugee policy), both destabilising for the region and a spur to the exploitation, and criminalisation, of some of the most vulnerable people on earth. The intention was to limit and ultimately prevent asylum seekers accessing refuge and, indeed, setting foot on Hungarian soil.

An imaginative criminological analysis that pays attention to space must also connect with the lived experience of those on the move, the 'losers' of globalisation, who must use the 'routes that fall foul of the normal regulatory systems' (Gyollai and Amatrudo, 2018: 1). The humiliation of people on the move, transgressing/crossing borders is writ large in the experiences and processes leading to migration, seeking asylum and refuge, and in the processes of settlement and belonging.

Marfleet (2006) argues 'that states have taken a calculated and instrumental approach to people who are vulnerable and often defenceless, and that this must be put on the record and challenged' (p xiii). This instrumental approach is evidenced in Adelman's historical analysis of the last three successive refugee regimes,[1] which are intrinsically related to processes of globalisation and modernity, and Massey's (2005) analysis of space, place and time. The three regimes are defined as: Population Exchange and Border Adjustments; International Humanitarian Protection; and The Age of the Camps. We argue here for a fourth regime, representative of current times: the Hardening of Borders.

In our previous book, we argued for the vitality of 'the art of thinking critically and creatively for developing and sustaining a criminological imagination' (O'Neill and Seal, 2012: 158). We called for critical, creative criminology to use innovative methodologies to better interpret and understand social issues and problems, as well as to deal with complexity and stereotypical thinking, and document the resistance and liveable lives of those who are marginalised and humiliated. In the following sections we examine each of these refugee regimes, the transgressions and emerging micropolitics through film, ethnographic, biographical and walking research methods and analysis

---

[1] Sales (2007) and Kofman et al (2000) use the concept of migration regime to explain migratory flows in specific historical contexts.

with a focus on key themes of micrology, space, time, place, memory and cultural memory.

Refugee regime 1: Population Exchanges and Border Adjustments

Adelman (1999) shows that the first regime emerged in the interwar years, between the First and Second World Wars and that 'population exchange and border adjustments became the major model for dealing with a refugee population' (p 90) linked to the creation and protection of nation states. The Greek-Turkish exchanges of 1922–3 are described as a consequence of the formation of nation states out of the disintegration of the Ottoman Empire and importantly, the Treaty of Lausanne, signed by the Allies, Greece and Turkey (Clark, 2006). The Lausanne peace treaty (which followed the failed Treaty of Sèvres) defined the borders of Turkey, Greece and Bulgaria, and established the independence of the republic of Turkey and the protection of the Muslim minority in Greece and the Christian minority in Turkey. As a result of the treaty 400,000 Muslims and 1.2 million Greek Orthodox Christians were forcibly moved from Turkey to Greece and vice versa.

This regime is identified by Adelman (1999) and Marfleet, (2006) not only as a moral failure on the part of western countries, but also as the failure of the nation state system. Adelman (1999) argues that the failure of the population exchange and border adjustment regime in the interwar years, which 'endorsed the right of nation states to exclude those attempting to enter their states as they fled persecution' (p 91) subsequently prevented 'all but a token number of Jews from obtaining sanctuary' from genocide and ethnic cleansing (p 91). As Clark (2007: xi) explains:

> Whether we like it or not, those of us who live in Europe or in places influenced by European ideas remain the children of Lausanne; that is to say, of the convention signed on a Swiss Lakeside after the First World War which decreed a massive, forced population movement between Turkey and Greece.

Clark (2007: 1) highlights that '[a]ll over Turkey and Greece, you can see the physical remnants of a world whose component parts seem to have been broken apart, suddenly and with great violence'. The Greek island of Chios faces Turkey and is a key point of rescue and arrival for thousands of migrants arriving in overcrowded boats. A watery border of around 12 kilometres separates Chios from Çesme across the Aegean on the Turkish coast. Chios is also a point of departure, a 'gateway to Europe and a better future' (O'Neill and Perivolaris, 2016, np).

In early summer 2016 Maggie O'Neill undertook a walking biography (O'Neill and Roberts 2019)) with John Perivolaris, a photographer based in the United Kingdom, born in Canada to migrant parents from Greece. The walking biography (as micrology) turned out also to be a biography of place, an unfolding history of the region and spatial politics; and in sociologist C. Wright Mills' (1959 cf 1970) terms, facilitated better understanding of the relationship between individual experience, private troubles and broader societal relationships, spaces, structures and histories.

Walking in Chios

Walking with John in Chios facilitated our sociological/criminological imagination. John stated that he wanted to undertake the walk because Chios is a "significant place" for him "in terms of my personal history and my family history" and it gave him an opportunity to think about memories that were "inherited from my family about Chios and also my own memories of the place, as well as my new impressions of Chios. The island has changed quite a lot since the last time I was here." One strong image and memory John shared at the start of the walk he describes as inherited from his father. His father had told him that when he was a little boy he used to stroll in the evenings with his grandfather (John's great-grandfather) along the town's coastal promenade, which faces Turkey.

> 'My father had a very close relationship with his grandfather, even closer than the one between himself and his father. They used to have long conversations on these walks. My dad must have been around ten, I imagine. My great-grandfather was elderly at that time. During these walks, they would talk. However, there was always one point along the walk where my great-grandfather would go completely silent and they would sit on the low wall that runs alongside the pavement. My great-grandfather would suddenly be lost for words. He'd just gaze out across the water to Çesme, the Turkish town opposite. He was an Edwardian-era gentleman, restrained in his manners. He would have frowned at anyone showing too much emotion.'

John went on to say that on a couple of occasions his father saw tears in his grandfather's eyes, silent tears.

> 'That image of tears got me thinking. I have this image in my mind of an old gentleman who had come to Chios as part of the exchange of populations in 1922 ... A typical experience shared by those who were exiled from their previous lives in Asia Minor ... Suddenly finding themselves Greek citizens, they had to adapt to a country they didn't know, after having lived in Asia Minor alongside Armenians, Turks, Jews, and others as part of the Ottoman world.'

John goes on to say that the political border between Greece and Turkey is fluid and it is 'historically layered and permeated by human loss and displacement, down to the current economic and refugee crises, along the fault line that divides but also joins the two countries. A salty border of sea and tears' (Perivolaris and O'Neill, 2016, np). For John, "trauma is the link with which borders are drawn on maps" and thinking in terms not only of images but of physical space he states that he welcomes the opportunity the walking project presents because it enables him to take a closer look at the layering of space, place and (family) history.

The next stop on the walk was a statue of General Plastiras on horseback facing across the Aegean Sea to Turkey, 'sword drawn and confronting the coast of Turkey' (O'Neill and Perivolaris, 2016, np). On the opposite shore is a statue of Kemal Ataturk, also facing across the Aegean Sea, sword drawn. "And, since 2009, in Buca Izmir, he has been dwarfed by a 132-foot relief sculpture on the scale of Mount Rushmore of Kemal Ataturk's head and bust" in the cliffs facing Chios. This, for John, is a "perfect illustration of the gendered confrontation out of which nations have all-too often been born". Indeed, this is also resonant in the dominance of the masculinist elements of representations and understandings of 'nation' (see Chapter 3).

During our walk, on day three, we met an aid worker who invited us into Souda Refugee Camp situated against the outer wall of the old town of Chios by the harbour. John tells us that the medieval town was initially constructed as a citadel by the Byzantines in the 10th century, that the surviving structure dates back to the 14th century, and was largely built by the Genoese, who ruled the island until the 16th century. It was then occupied by the Ottoman Turks until 1922, with the exception of its six-month occupation by the Venetians in 1694. Post-1922, it was largely occupied by Greek refugees from Asia

Minor, including the maternal side of his family, and the current refugee camp, next to the walls of the medieval citadel, is yet another chapter of the refugee experience on an island of refugees (O'Neill and Perivolaris and, 2016, np).

The refugee camp is a liminal space butted up against the old wall, next to the harbour and the town's main square, with its small park, town hall and a section of small cafes. Discussing the spatial layout John remarked that this view of the square could tell the viewer about another border or frontier social class. The square and long narrow park behind it marks a border. On one side are the working class cafes and behind them the medieval citadel and refugee camp. On the opposite side, is the town's main shopping avenue and the former house of John's great-grandfather (now a bank): 'The contrast between the sides of the square tells you everything you need to know about class. The square and park mark the frontier between middle-class Chios and working-class Chios' (O'Neill and Perivolaris, 2016, np).

Looking down towards the camp from this vantage point a fence runs along the far edge of the camp. On the town side, the official United Nations High Commissioner for Refugees (UNHCR) tents are situated, a makeshift school, toilets, showers and clinics. On the other side of the fence are improvised tents made by the refugees themselves from donated materials, cardboard and shreds of discarded UNHCR tents; a kind of shantytown. The camp is hemmed in on one side by the walled town and the sea, and, on this side, by the main road going to the north of the island. The camp forms a strip made up of the main camp and its shanty suburb.

We walked through a line of tents on the left and a wire fence on the right, behind which was another line of tents. Washing had been hung to dry on the fence. Many of these tents were makeshift, with UNHCR material, sheeting and the blue cloth of the 'Samaritan's Purse' charity. We walked past the toilet blocks and the showers all in a row and a water point with large sinks. Water was freely available for drinking and there were phone-charging points too. Near to the water point was a small structure where an aid agency was supporting new mothers and their babies We stopped by a large map of the camp that told the resident where they were in Greece.

While talking to aid workers our attention was caught by a crowd and we were joined by a husband and wife with their baby, who told us that a young man, an amputee, had jumped into the sea in an attempt to swim back to Turkey. We were told that because he swam from Turkey to Chios and did not arrive by boat the officials could not or would not 'process him'. The day before we had seen the young man looking agitated, pacing about on crutches. The mother asked us: "Why do we have to wait here? It has been eight months. Why can't we go on. This is terrible. My daughter is sick, she has scabs on her lips."

The camp was a holding place, a space of containment and indeed confinement, for those who had transgressed various nation states' borders, including the watery border in front of us. The evidence of the stasis of confinement is made clear in this conversation – the interminable wait, in time and space – and its impact. Geographers have drawn attention to the way these spaces of containment control mobility, particularly through the 'growth of detention in transit' (Conlon et al, 2017: 3). International organisations and Nation states fund and support a developing 'enforcement infrastructure' of containment that operate as 'buffer zones turned processing spaces', indeed, 'holding pens for migrants' (Levy, 2015 quoted in Conlon et al, 2017). What is clear in the available literature is that 'transit has become increasingly prolonged and fragmented for migrants' (Conlon et al, 2017: 3; Collyer, 2010).

The aid worker tells us that women were choosing formula milk rather than breast milk, as due to stress their milk had dried up. This was creating further health problems because formula needs to be mixed with water and is not as clean as breast milk. They were joined by another aid worker who told them that a young man who had tried to commit suicide in the camp was returned from hospital to the same tent where this had happened, thus placing him in the same circumstances that had led to his suicide attempt. After two days back in the camp he successfully requested to be returned to Turkey. The aid workers identified several pressing needs, including translators and interpreters, food donations, social media campaigning, and lobbying of European politicians. A further issue of concern is the risk of burn-out for aid workers living and working in these spaces of containment, working on the front line, dealing with the micro realities and impact of negative globalisation.

On leaving the camp, our conversation was focused on the material, symbolic and intra psychic borders they experienced there, the borders between people and the watery fluid border in front of their very eyes, where the young amputee had attempted his desperate swim back to Turkey. Walking along the strip of land bordering the sea and the town, a place where people waited in limbo for their claims to be processed, they were surrounded by historical layering of previous migrations, in the walls and stones of the old town, constructed from fragments of ancient Greek, Byzantine Ottoman and Genoese buildings.

The concept of 'negative globalisation' aptly describes the connections between the stories w had heard, their lived, sensory experiences and the relationship to broader social issues and politics. We were struck by the horror of hearing about the young man who could not be 'processed' by the 'administrative-material functions of the state' (Benhabib, 2004: 4) and so in the 'margins of the margins' (Agamben, 1995) he attempts to swim back across the border of water that is the Aegean Sea, a sea that is patrolled by border forces.

The walk enabled Maggie to connect with the micrology of John's biography, cultural history and familial experiences of the 'population exchanges' and the long, turbulent history of refugee and forced migration to/from Greece and Turkey as well as the current humanitarian and refugee crisis and austerity politics. It also enabled her to understand something of the biography of the island through the spaces, landmarks and places that were important to John. Sitting under a large photograph of people arriving on boats in 1922/23 in a café, John asks:

> 'From where is it possible to begin? All Greeks are used to living among ruins, even those, like me, who are offspring of two diasporas: the exchange of populations after the end of the Ottoman Empire, and second great diaspora after World War Two. The latter scattered Greeks to several countries and continents, primarily to the United States and Australia and, in my case, England. How is it possible to present a continuous narrative out of diaspora, when diaspora involves interruption, a shattering of history, biography, and identity? ... Borders offer limits but also invite us to exceed those limits.'

The impact of the population exchanges and border adjustments are played out in the transgressive acts, border crossings and in the cultural memory and current geography of the border – the place near the old town wall and harbour where generations of forced migrations, of refugees have been situated, contained, confined and who wait. The micrology of lived lives is told, in part, through John's biography and ethnographic walk in Souda camp. Here the traces of the past are experienced and felt by John – in the liminal space of the camp.

Refugee regime 2: International Humanitarian Protection

The second regime emerged after the Second World War, and Holocaust, with the introduction of the International Refugee

Convention in 1951 (for European refugees only, followed by the 1967 protocol that made the convention universal). Here borders remained intact and convention refugees were recognised as needing and having the right to the protection of a state. The development of an international 'global and political humanitarian regime' (Adelman, 1999: 98) involved either return to the state from which the person had fled; settlement in the country of first asylum; or resettlement in other countries. However, Adelman's (1999) analysis stated that access to refugee determination was limited and increasingly restrictionist policies emerged to respond to refugees from the South seeking entry to countries of the North.

The second regime was based on the rights of individuals to protection who had a 'well founded fear of persecution' and were outside the borders of their country. This was made up of two types of protection: 'obligatory' for any state that signed the convention and as a 'voluntary' system for dealing with large numbers fleeing for reasons other than individual persecution. For example, the people who fled the oppressive governments of Uganda in 1972, Chile in 1973 and Iran in 1979 were 'resettled as humanitarian refugees rather than as convention refugees by a voluntary system of resettlement' (Adelman, 1999: 94). This regime began to falter as the number of refugees increased and Benhabib (2004) argues that the situation gives rise to a major contradiction between, on the one hand, universal human rights and, on the other, restrictionist and protective state policies. Drawing on Benhabib (1994), O'Neill (2010) writes that the growing paradox between international human rights norms, especially the rights of migrants, refugees and asylum seekers, and 'assertions of territorial sovereignty' (p 7) marks out the current situation of a 'world of increasingly deterritorialized politics' (p 11). And as Adelman (1999: 93) points out, refugees turned out to be the 'Achilles' heel of the system'.

The increase in measures to prevent entry, tighter visa requirements and sanctions against carriers carrying passengers who lack travel documentation combine to create a 'hostile' environment for migrants (Liberty, 2018). At one end of the spectrum is statelessness, a loss of rights and in Benhabib's (2004) terms a loss of the right to have rights. The exclusionary policy led to the third regime, keeping refugees in their own or neighbouring countries, the 'era of regional solutions' and the age of the camps. This loss of the right to have rights is further expounded in Mbembe's (2003) work on necropolitics, building on Foucault's concept of bio-power. The ultimate impact of negative globalisation, of restrictionist and protective state policies in a world of 'deterritorialized politics' is not only the containment and confinement of people in camps, the transgression of the 1951 Refugee Convention, but also the power over who shall live or die – what Mbembe (2000, 2003) calls 'necropolitics'.

Necropolitics

The social and in many cases actual death experienced by those in the 'state of exception', 'outside the normal state of law' beyond citizenship, at the margins of the margins (Agamben, 1995) is evidenced in the following example. In the first seven months of 2018 '1,600 people were known to have died or gone missing in the Mediterranean Sea and along land routes'. This figure excludes people who died 'along routes to and through North Africa, such as in the Sahara Desert or Libya'; 1,100 of these deaths were 'at sea along the Central Mediterranean route'. The report states that the increasing death rates were due in part to 'decreased search and rescue off the Libyan coast' (UNHCR, 2018: 11). In 2014, at the height of the 'crisis', the British government withdrew from offering planned search and resource operations in the Mediterranean. In the words of Baroness Anelay of St Johns, Minister of State in the Foreign and Commonwealth Office, this was because "We do not support planned search and rescue operations in the Mediterranean. We believe that they create an unintended 'pull factor', encouraging more migrants to attempt the dangerous sea crossing and thereby leading to more tragic and unnecessary deaths."

The UK government focused instead on border control via Operation Triton. At this time, Maurice Wren, CEO of the Refugee Council, said:

'The British Government seems oblivious to the fact that the world is in the grip of the greatest refugee crisis since the Second World War. People fleeing atrocities will not stop coming if we stop throwing them life rings; boarding a rickety boat in Libya will remain a seemingly rational decision if you're running for your life and your country is in flames. The only outcome of withdrawing help will be to witness more people needlessly and shamefully dying on Europe's doorstep. The answer isn't to build the walls of fortress Europe higher, it's to provide more safe and legal channels for people to access protection.'

International Humanitarian Protection, it seems, is a thing of the past, replaced for some by necropolitics and for others a life lived in a refugee camp.

Refugee regime 3: The Age of the Camps

The third regime involves a 'regional solution' – containing people in camps and thus preventing mass movement, as this is interpreted as 'dangerous and destabilising' (Marfleet, 2006). There are many examples of this regime: Dadaab camp in Kenya; Palestinian refugee camps in Lebanon, Jordan and Syria; Syrian camps in Jordan. In Jordan, Lebanon, Syria and Kenya some people have lived their whole lives, have been born and died in the camp, originally a temporary solution. The Palestinian camps were opened after the 1948 Arab-Israeli war. Yarmouk Palestinian camp in Syria on the outskirts of Damascus was opened in 1957 as an 'unofficial' camp; it is the largest Palestinian camp in Syria. The population was estimated at 18,000 in 2015, and following devastation by Islamic state forces by the time the Syrian government took control, the population was estimated at 100–200 people in 2018.

Adelman states that the UNHCR has evolved from an agency that sought to protect refugees to being the largest relief agency 'organised to serve refugees and displaced persons' (Adelman, 1999: 100). Tassioglou and Dobrowlesky (2006) write that Dadaab camp in Kenya was created 100km from the Somali/Kenya border in 1991 and in 2006, 130,000 of the initial 400,000 Somali refugees remained in Dadaab, prohibited to leave the area without 'special permits from the United Nations High Commissioner for Refugees (UNHCR) the main organization administering the camps' (Abdi, 2006: 233). The social harm perpetrated against women in the camp is particularly distressing. Their non-citizenship is an important factor in the risks and insecurity they suffer as well as gender-based violence, including rape (Tassioglou and Dobrowlesky, 2006: Abdi, 2006).

Although Kenya is a signatory to both the UN Convention on Human Rights and the Organisation on African Unity (OAU) Convention on Refugees, it has taken a hands off approach to its refugee population. 'Even after 10 years in Kenya, the government still maintains that Somali refugees are aliens in transit, thereby refusing to extend legal rights to them' (Abdi, 2006: 246). The 'global realities that stem from the intricate interplay of gender, migration and citizenship, and the inclusions and exclusions that result under specific conditions' (Tassioglou and Dobrowlesky, 2006: 4) are expressed very starkly in the 'non-citizen' position of Somali refugee women in the Dadaab camp.

At night, the *shiftas* just enter your house. You are sitting among your children and a gunman enters. There is nothing he can do if he wants to, he will rape you if he pleases, he will rob you of the rations you have collected that day, if he pleases. And the children are without food the next day. (Abdi 2006: 238)

Yarmouk Camp: Blue

In the film *Blue* (Gabi, 2014) by the director Abo Gabi, and produced by Bidayyat and Rad Fael, the director, having fled Yarmouk camp for Beirut, tells a story about Yarmouk and the suffering there through a documentary film based around his friend Ayham, who wheels his piano through the streets, stopping to play at various places and singing with the crowds that gather – songs of lament and resistance. The context to this resilient, resistant spirit of the Palestinian refugees in Yarmouk is a nightmarish, dystopian environment of burned-out, shelled buildings and utter devastation. When watching the film one can almost taste the dust in the atmosphere, the lack of water and sanitation.

The director writes:

> I've had a recurring dream since I fled the Yarmouk Refugee Camp and came to Beirut. The dream takes me back to besieged Yarmouk, where death and destruction have found a way to settle in all its details. I am not sure whether it is a dream or a nightmare. But I live in this open-ended waiting with images of that place and the difficulty of abandoning it. Maybe the sound of my friend Ayham's piano changed the nightmare into dream and the place into a legend. Here, there is no geography, a place between two times, the first is a tent and the second is bags packed for other conquests. These conquests stimulate the hardness and bitterness of our catastrophes and previous disappointments. We pack our luggage to find only our memory that tells the stories of our relation with the wind. We, as witnesses of disappointment and hope. (Gabi, 2014: np)

The film is called *Blue* because in the dream everything is blue. There are no more birds in the trees – they have fed the hungry children of Yarmouk. We see a funeral procession, mourners filling the streets carrying a body wrapped in white cloths, the 80th person to die of starvation in the 450-day siege of Yarmouk. While Ayham plays, the men around the piano sing:

> time goes on just like everyday,
> the night is trying to fall asleep,
> the night searches for some sleep,
> its become quite a long time,
> the moon is incomplete,
> and time goes on,
> my pain becomes water.

At the end of this song someone says, 'Quickly guys, let's get out of here before a mortar falls.' *Blue* represents the camp of Yarmouk from the lived experience of those who live there and is a clear example of this third refugee regime as well as an attempt to document and represent lived lives through the transgressive/resistant playing of the piano at various spaces in the camp devastated by bombing. The film is also an example (and reminder) of cultural memory. Both *Blue* and the feminist research conducted in Dadaab bring to light issues of statelessness, lack of citizenship, the lack of a right to have rights; as well as the resistance of the people living in the camp to exclusionary structures, discourses and practices, seeking to make liveable lives in the contained (confined) space of the camp. The image of the piano being wheeled through the streets and people emerging and gathering to sing is a transgressive act, a 'punctum' (Barthes, 1981); it pierces the viewer and connects us with the lives and experiences of those in the camp in ways we cannot forget.

Refugee regime 4: A Hardening of Borders

The regime currently in process represents a pinning down and hardening of borders and the reinforcement of 'regional solutions'. Examples include: the fence in Hungary; the 'hostile environment' (Liberty, 2018) in the United Kingdom (and, in part, the 'yes' vote in the UK exit referendum); Donald Trump's rhetoric of 'building a wall' in the United States and the shocking separation and internment of migrant parents from their children; the camps in Greece, and the 11.5km triple wire fence that separates the city of Mellila (a Spanish and thus EU enclave in Morocco) from the migrants/refugees attempting to access 'Europe'. Mathis Kispert's film *No More Beyond* (2015) is indicative of refugee regime 4 and tells a story in three parts, using three screens, interviews with migrants, poetry, documentary film making and journalism. *No More Beyond* is a space open to the future without the possibility of entry –'non plus ultra'.

The film represents borders 'not just as the line of separation, but also at the threshold where the violence that sustains inequality erupts and is forcibly revealed' (Kispert, 2015). In one scene a migrant asks: 'What is the legal way to immigrate? Why don't they give me this option? I am illegal because there is no legal route' (Kispert, 2015). The film also shows that people smuggling is a consequence of borders in the context of both negative globalisation and the flow of capital, goods and trade. A key trope in the film is borders as sites of struggle that have, following DeCerteau (1985), both fragmented and complex histories. Juxtaposed with images of the mountains of West Africa and a golf course situated just beyond the Melilla crossing fence we learn that one man has lived for 13 months on the mountain. He says, "I have courage, friends have died at the borders – it is a big risk – I have had three months without a shower because of the cold." His feet are scarred and the message is clear, that migration, as an act of transgression and criminalisation, creates criminals, who are punished, who are maimed or who die trying to reach 'beyond' – 'non plus ultra'.

The film provides a good example of visual research and visual culture that documents and represents lived experiences, claims a space for the voices of the unnamed, raises awareness of the social harms, relations of humiliation, exclusion and challenges exclusionary processes and practices. *No More Beyond* creates space for the articulation of identity and belonging for those situated in the asylum–migration nexus through the ethnographic storytelling. This is vitally important to the development of dialogue and recognition of experience and social justice for migrants whose voices and experiences are usually mediated by others, notably the mainstream press and media.

Arendt (1994) states that 'one's status as a rights-bearing person is contingent on the recognition of one's membership' and she identified 'the twin phenomena of "political evil" and "statelessness"' as the most daunting problems of the 20th and 21st centuries (see also Benhabib, 2004: 50). Statelessness for Arendt meant loss of citizenship and loss of rights, indeed the loss of citizenship meant the loss of rights altogether. In *Transgressive Imaginations* (2012) we argued that we need to face up to our global responsibilities towards the displaced, address the causes of 'the misery of growing refugee movements' and foster dignity and egalisation (Lindner, 2006) in the institutions, laws, policies and practices towards people seeking safety in the asylum–migration nexus. In 2019 the situation is much worse: asylum seekers and refugees have become the folk devils of the 21st century, with the mass movement of people across borders a key defining feature of what Zygmunt Bauman called 'negative' or 'uneven' globalisation (Bauman, 2004) marked by 'wasted lives' and, as we document above in Refugee regime 2, 'necropolitics' (Mbembe, 2003).

Increasingly restrictive asylum policies impact on the humiliation and social marginalisation of people seeking asylum as well as those who have lived in the United Kingdom for a lifetime and call it their home, fuelling racism and race hatred. There is an urgent need to challenge and transform the social harms perpetrated against migrants. This is particularly important given the context of: conflict, war, migration surges; the withdrawal of humanising practices and a lack of welcome to people seeking asylum by European states; a heightening of the adversarial approach to those who seek to make their lives in the United Kingdom and the North; and the hardening of Europe's borders. At the same time, as many commentators have stated, there is an astonishing lack of accountability and responsibility by governments and states for their part in the production of the world's refugees and in an age of glocal and globalisation, sovereignty is vigorously asserted at the borders of nations.

What can we as imaginative criminologists do, how can we apply or operationalise our critical theory and methods? Methodologically, participatory and participatory arts research, as micrology, as part of a public criminology, can help to build communities of practice to challenge and change such gross inequalities and open and keep open spaces for critical thinking, mobilising resistance, recognition and respect for people migrating – people moving beyond war, violence, poverty and environmental disasters (O'Neill, 2010). This, for us, is part of the democratic potential and promise of critical and cultural criminology and a central reason for our research collaborations with artists, writers and asylum/refugee/migrant communities. Underpinned by the principles of inclusion, participation, valuing all voices and developing action-oriented interventions, participatory, collaborative research is a process and a practice directed towards social change; it is interventionist, action oriented and interpretive. It offers a micropolitics as transgressive, as change causing, with an openness to the future. Fals Borda (1999) writes about the challenges of developing a more holistic epistemology that facilitates researchers taking a moral stand while also balancing the ideal and the possible. We argue that creative and imaginative research can offer multi-sensory, dialogic and visual routes to understanding and can often say what cannot be said in words alone – can *say the unsayable and non-conceptual*. We have argued that arts-based research is central to countering exclusionary processes and practices and can generate greater knowledge and understanding as well as delivering on 'social justice' by facilitating a radical democratic imaginary. By the latter we mean, following Smith (1998), to open and keep open space for repressed elements of the imaginary, for a democratic imaginary (O'Neill and Seal, 2012).

As we stated in Chapter 1, there is limited awareness or critical reflection on understanding space and place in criminological research. In this chapter we have sought to address this by examining four successive refugee regimes and analysing the importance of space through the relational, embodied and imagined experiences of migrants and the material and symbolic concept of transgression and the border and border spaces in their lives, journeys and sense of belonging; albeit for many, confined, contained in the camps.

In the next chapter, we continue our focus on the themes of borders and cultural memory by discussing issues of space, place, violence and transgression uncovered in arts-based participatory and ethnographic and walking research (micrology) conducted in Canada and Northern Ireland.

6

Imagining Spaces of Violence and Transgression in Vancouver and Northern Ireland

In Chapter 5 we discussed responses to migration across four distinct regimes; the making of liminal in-between spaces in the form of camps for the displaced, in Bauman's terms 'human waste'; and the usefulness of a threefold analysis of space through the relational, embodied and imagined experiences of migrants. In Chapter 6 we build on this analysis by examining the social dynamics and the visual and material culture of urban space *as well as* the embodied, relational and imagined/lived experience of public space in two cities, Vancouver, Canada and Belfast, Northern Ireland. We focus specifically on two areas of each city, the Downtown Eastside (DTES) in Vancouver, also known as 'skid row', and central and central/north Belfast, where the 'peace lines' and 'peace walls' separate, demarcate and act as borders between two communities of Belfast's citizens.

In Chapter 6 we focus specifically on the issue of space, place, violence and transgression, drawing on these two case studies in Vancouver and Belfast. 'Imagining spaces of violence and transgression in Vancouver and Northern Ireland' focuses first of all on the lives of indigenous women and sex workers in Vancouver's DTES and then explores the 'architecture of conflict' in the 'peace walls', 'peace lines' or 'border lines' in Belfast in the context of spaces of war, violence and conflict. For 26 years on 14 February, Valentine's Day, women of the DTES have led a Memorial March through the city, stopping at the places and spaces where women were murdered or went missing. We draw on material from walking methods, photographs and interviews with women who attended the march in 2016 to examine spaces of past, present and future in their lives. Arts-based walking methods are also utilised that explore the peace walls, peace lines and interfaces as border spaces through sensory multi-modal research.

We suggest, drawing on Ash Amin's work, that the 'convivial commons' we experienced walking with residents in the Downtown Eastside of Vancouver and Belfast offers a good example of what might be called on the one hand a 'successful public space' with various opportunities to participate in communal activity (Amin, 2006: 1), despite the media messages and public perceptions about the two sites, particularly the DTES. On the other hand, however, the material impact of poverty, austerity, violence (and sectarianism in Belfast) complicates this, with the impact of poverty more visually apparent in the DTES. Moreover, the impact of poverty and stigma in the DTES and sectarianism in Belfast has a clear impact on the well-being of both communities.

The DTES is perceived as edgy, risky and dangerous and at the time of our ethnographic research it was suggested on tourist websites that visitors should keep out of this area and certainly not go there after dark. On tourist websites Belfast is documented as a safe city to visit but the *Lonely Planet* guide suggests tourists avoid 'the so-called "interface areas" – near the peace lines in West Belfast, Crumlin Rd and the Short Strand (just east of Queen's Bridge) – after dark. If in doubt about any area, ask at your hotel or hostel' (Lonely Planet, 2018, np).

The guide informs readers that they will notice a 'more obvious security presence than elsewhere in the UK and Ireland, such as armoured police Land Rovers and fortified police stations. There are doormen on many city-centre pubs.' Moreover, 'dissident Republican groups continue a campaign of violent attacks aimed at police and military targets but have very little public support'. Visitors are recommended to follow the police service of Northern Ireland on twitter for alerts and updates (Lonely Planet, 2018, np).

An important point to make is that our knowledge, understanding and experience of both city spaces was gained through walking with local residents while undertaking participatory, arts-based ethnographic research. The historical, relational, material, embodied and sensory affordances that this research allowed are instrumental in supporting and evidencing our arguments here.

In critical analyses of urban public space a number of relevant themes emerge that connect to our experiences of both sites, such as: the importance of enabling sociability and community, building in the possibility that 'people must encounter one another in person' (Jacobs, 2005: 37), including the diverse groups that share neighbourhoods and city spaces; and managing public space to facilitate engagement with others (Amin, 2006: 1). More recently Amin (2013) has offered the concept of 'telescopic urbanism' to acknowledge a shift from a top-down focus on the economics and governance of the urban city to a more welfare-based or human rights, humanitarian and grass roots approach that also means the 'urban poor' are involved in changes to transform their lives. In response Datta (2013) argues that 'rights cannot be realised only through top-down political imperatives or gargantuan social engineering models,' nor 'subaltern resistance and social organisation among the urban poor against the state' rather, her 'third way' is developed from her work in the global South, in 'the context of a rising culture of legality enforced by the state'. Datta (2013) argues 'that for much of the urban poor, the politics around the right to the city is often focused on a politics of entitlement that is based on concrete and symbolic encounters with law in urban spaces'. Datta's argument is particularly relevant to the experience of marginalised, indigenous communities in DTES.

However, in his earlier work, Amin (2006: 1) also argues that people's use of public space, parks, libraries, streets and squares is 'more likely to be interpreted in terms of their impact on cultures of consumption, practices of negotiating the urban environment, and social response to anonymous others, than in terms of their centrality in shaping civic and political culture'. Amin suggests, addressing the themes of collective culture and urban public space, that 'in an age of urban sprawl, multiple usage of public space and proliferation of the sites of political and cultural expression, it seems odd to expect public spaces to fulfill their traditional role as spaces of civic inculcation and political participation' (p 1). We understand Amin's point here to be questioning the possibilities for public space to offer 'opportunities to participate in communal activity', indeed sociability, connected to civic culture, civic practices and participation because of the distributed, plural and even disembedded nature of our face-to-face encounters with others in urban and public space.

Urban planning is defined, in one sense, as an attempt to manage public space to enable engagement with others and build sociability (Amin, 2006). However, another way of looking at urban space beyond the development and management of urban public space as a proving ground for sociability that supports 'civic and political citizenship' includes the emergent properties of space and place – what space and place might signify and facilitate in our two sites. A very important dimension to include in our analysis is that of time, related to the quickening aspect of social life, which Rosa (2013) calls 'social acceleration' and Vostal (2016) 'the temporal dynamics of capitalism'.

Thinking about these temporal and spatial themes through a creative, sociological/criminological lens means we must also pay attention to the historical use and meaning of space and to activities and practices that have taken place there, to unpack the cultural meaning and use of time/space/place; the operation of laws/legality; the impact of regeneration; and the 'temporal dynamics of capitalism' (Vostal, 2016). In the next section we focus on two sites, two urban public spaces in two cities, to explore the connections between space, place and time and the shaping of civic and public culture, especially in the light of the impact of violence and transgression experienced in both sites. In our analysis a strong theme of resistance emerged, gained through walking and connecting with the spaces and places of public and urban space through the lived lives of our co-walkers; for example, campaigns to challenge and change laws that were seen as punitive and unjust, as well as a demand for recognition and plenty of evidence of civic and political participation in both Vancouver and Belfast. Cultural memory and also well-being emerge as key themes.

Walking in the Downtown Eastside: the missing and murdered women's Memorial March

In February 2016 Maggie visited Vancouver to walk with Kerry Porth at the 26th annual Missing Women's Memorial March. In Vancouver, every 14 February, friends and family members as well as community groups and other citizens are led by indigenous women on a memorial march through the DTES, where they stop at sites where women died or were last seen, to offer prayers, medicines and roses in remembrance. The WordPress website dedicated to documenting the march and sharing news and information says the following:

> The first women's memorial march was held in 1992 in response to the murder of a woman on Powell Street in Vancouver. Out of this sense of hopelessness and anger came an annual march on Valentine's Day to express compassion, community, and caring for all women in Vancouver's Downtown Eastside, Unceded Coast Salish Territories.
>
> The women's memorial march continues to honour the lives of missing and murdered women and all women's lives lost in the Downtown Eastside. Increasing deaths of many vulnerable women from the DTES still leaves family, friends, loved ones, and community members with an overwhelming sense of grief and loss. Indigenous women disproportionately continue to go missing or be murdered with minimal to no action to address these tragedies or the systemic nature of gendered violence, poverty, racism, or colonialism. (Women's Memorial March, 2016, np)

The march draws attention to the murdered and missing women from the DTES who are indigenous, poor, including women who sell sex, use drugs and are homeless or living in hostels and shelters. The march is associated with the history of the DTES victims of serial killer Robert Pickton[1] as well as the political resistance by women in DTES to violence. More recently it has been associated with campaigns to challenge the laws around sex work, arguing for decriminalisation, constitutional challenges and resistance to the Protection of Communities and Exploited Persons Act C 36, which became law in November 2014. This law criminalised those who purchase sex, and in so doing, sex worker rights advocates state that this reduces the safety of women by increasing the risk of criminalisation for their clients. Violence against women, marginalised women and sex workers, many of whom were indigenous, is still a central issue for the communities in DTES, 26 years after the first march.

Robert Pickton, a pig farmer, was found guilty and convicted of the murder of six women, with clear evidence of the murder of a further 20 women from the DTES. Their bodies were dismembered and fed to his pigs. He eventually confessed to the murder of 49 women. A report published by the Royal Canadian Mounted Police in 2014 'put the total of missing and murdered aboriginal women at 1,181. Although indigenous women make up 4.3% of the Canadian population, the report found they account for 16% of female homicides and 11.3% of missing women.' The significance of these figures in highlighting the sexual violence and disposability of marginalised and indigenous women is shocking and tragic. As John Lowman argues, long-term criminalisation plays a key role in the continuum of violence committed against sex workers, in what he describes as 'deadly inertia' on the part of the state and criminal justice agencies (Lowman, 1987; 2000; 2011).

We covered a lot of ground in the walk and not only regarding the evolution and politics of the march, but in connecting the march to the bigger picture of violence against indigenous women and sex workers in Canada. The march itself is a memorial and memorialisation, a reminder and a symbol of protest and resistance. The start and close of the walk is marked by a healing circle, the rituals (sweetgrass and laying of roses), the colours and banners, traditional blankets and clothing, the drumming and women's warrior song all add to the rhythm of the walk, the walking, stopping, remembering, all are a reminder of our social connectedness.

---

[1] See: http://www.cbc.ca/news/canada/british-columbia/pickton-inquiry-accused-of-failing-marginalized-women-1.194869.

The route starts outside the Carnegie Center (Figure 6.1), a central and important landmark in the DTES, a place for community socialising, using the library, theatre and café, and attending classes. It is an open and welcoming public space. The march finishes with a healing circle at Oppenheimer Park around three hours later and there is also a community feast at the Japanese Language Hall.

The ability to move freely around the city, to take and hold space, is an important aspect of the missing women's march, an assertion of the right to the city and space, transgressing the borders and boundaries of stigma, race, and sexual and social inequalities, and at the same time calling attention to these in women's lives and especially the lives of indigenous women.

On the day of the march it is pouring with rain. Everyone is handed heart-shaped flags with the name of a woman, missing or dead, written very carefully onto the hearts. Everyone holds their hearts up around the circle. Some women are holding banners. Kerry tells us: 'the hearts are new this year and the banner in front of us, the panels were either sewn by women at the Women's Centre or by family members and so they're representing each of the serial killer victims' (Porth and O'Neill, 2016, np).

Figure 6.1: Walkers gather at the Carnegie Center, DTES at the start of the march

Image: Maggie O'Neill

At the various landmarks where a woman was last seen or found, sweetgrass is burnt and offerings are made to remember her, a rose is left in the place. Some of the stores and services to residents of the DTES close for the day (Figure 6.2).

The conversations along the route drew our attention to regeneration taking place in the area as we walked past a 'Versace at Home' store (very near the PACE sex work support organisation and a well-known hostel) and residents of the DTES talked about galloping (rather than creeping) regeneration, with displacement of community members articulated in the media as 'cleaning up of the area'. Kerry talked about both the movement into the community of 'young hipster professionals who think it's edgy to live down here' and 'the displacement of the people who call this place home and who have been here for so long feel that they're being displaced, and this community has such a long history of displacement for its indigenous people' (O'Neill and Porth,

Figure 6.2: Support services close for the day

Image: Maggie O'Neill

2016). The people we spoke to shared examples of extreme wealth in the area, such as 'a million dollars' worth of vehicles parked in a one block radius' and 'shoppers wearing their wealth ostentatiously' and the stark contrast with the visible poverty and health problems. They tell us that the unlicensed street market along Hastings Street has been cleaned out and moved away and how this has impacted on the sense of community and sociability.

> Yes, and in the last couple of months they had the police patrolling where the unofficial market in front of United has always been and I love it, it always reminds me of being in Africa actually, because it's like you have people fixing the bikes all the way to people selling whatever. And it's a need, like somebody only has two dollars but they have needs that need to be met, and they can't go into a regular store. The police were there to get them to leave otherwise you risk being arrested or ticketed and whatnot. So, there was one day I walked home from work and it was maybe four or five in the evening which usually it's pretty busy even on a rainy day, it was dead, just me and the police. (Jessica in Porth and O'Neill, 2016, np)

Issues of space, place, violence and transgression are writ large in the DTES and especially through the liminal status of the area, perceived as edgy, risky and dangerous. In *Transgressive Imaginations* we discussed a British Academy-funded ethnography undertaken by O'Neill and Stenning (2014) in 2010–11 using participatory arts and walking methods in the DTES. The research used arts-based methods, walking and photography to examine 'community' and the way it was experienced, understood, imagined and documented through the eyes of the inhabitants – the binners, sex workers, street vendors and artists struggling to make out in circumstances not of their choosing.[2]

---

[2] This research project (O'Neill and Stenning September 2010–September 2011) was funded by the British Academy, the Wolfson Research Institute and the School of Applied Social Sciences, Durham University). The project sought to explore, in partnership with local agencies, ways of seeing the spaces and places of community through the eyes of DTES residents and workers, using participatory action research (PAR) and participatory arts (PA). This research built upon Stenning's photographs of DTES in 2002 and 2008. The principles underpinning PAR and PA are: inclusion, participation, valuing all local voices, community-driven and sustainable outcomes. Community co-researchers based in each organisation worked with Maggie O'Neill

One dominant theme in the research was the struggle for recognition and the way this emerged against depictions that categorise and record residents as abject, 'other' and 'different'. We argued, using Barthes' (1981) notion of the 'punctum', that certain photographs and social media, visual methodologies, photographs, gathered through participatory and arts-based research, can pierce us and facilitate access to the liveable lives of the residents made out in the margins of the city and the margins of legality, welfare and poverty. What unfolded through the stories of residents told in both narrative and in images challenged the rather simplistic message of the 'deviant' inhabitants and criminality of the residents of 'skid row' found in the mainstream media. They tell instead about the social struggle and the resistance involved in their everyday lives and the many ways they challenge hegemonic images that define them as abject and 'othered' (O'Neill and Seal, 2012). At that time, welfare benefits were around $500 per month and the cheapest single room in DTES cost $375 and so people survived by using the food banks and missions provided by various organisations and were able to get free (recycled) clothing from agencies, such as the DTES Neighbourhood Center and women's centres. Some of the people we spoke to at that time were sleeping in shelters or on the streets but overwhelmingly there was a strong sense of belonging to the DTES community and a desire for this to be recognised.

In the intervening years, police action and regeneration were changing the area, reducing the numbers of poorer community members out on the street and increasing the visibility of 'hipsters', wealthy residents and business owners. The issues of space, place and the social acceleration of capitalism and gentrification were plain to see; the very presence of a Versace at Home store in the DTES was a significant landmark and marker. The cultures of consumption and the operation of capital combined to displace the poorer residents, those marked as 'out of place' and indeed 'disposable'. Yet, at one and the same time, public space, the spaces and places of 'community', for the marginalised residents of the DTES are visibly claimed as 'sites of political and cultural expression' through interventions such as the Missing Women's Memorial March. This is a temporal space 'of civic inculcation and political participation' (Amin, 2006: 1) and now a deeply embedded marker of cultural memory in the DTES. Now

to conduct the research and supported the creation of visual representations of 'community'. This group formed the research team and authored the report and articles.

in its 28th year the impact of the march is slow but steady; a new consultation has been launched to examine the issues, with centre stage given to the notion that black and indigenous and marginalised women's lives matter. Given the reality of real estate value of the area, situated right next to Gastown and Chinatown, near to the harbour and a walk away from the business and banking district, our fear is, drawing on Rosa (2013) and Vostal (2016), that 'the temporal dynamics of capitalism' will in time erase the poorer communities in the DTES and they will be but a trace referenced in the fact that these are Coast Salish lands.

The peace lines and interface areas in Belfast

Four walks were undertaken in Belfast in 2016 that enabled an understanding of Belfast linked to the history of conflict, the 'Troubles' and what Michael Conlon, one of the co-walkers, called 'the architecture of conflict'. We focus here on one ethnographic walk. The walk with Michael was from central Belfast. We met at the Europa Hotel, towards North Belfast and the New Lodge Road, 'a large, Nationalist Republican area, dominated with seven towers, multi-storey tower blocks, a lot of poverty, a lot of social deprivation but it was also a very, very strong area of resistance' (O'Neill and Conlon, 2016: np). Michael spoke about the changing shape of the city, which is, in part, impacted by the peace process and by the process of conflict transformation. He said, 'It is part of the process of conflict transformation, that you respect the history and you understand it and especially for the families who have to live with it every day, that there's somebody not sitting in an armchair, there's somebody not sitting at the kitchen table and that's where the lead is really, from the families' (O'Neill and Conlon, 2016: np).

Blown up three times and shot twice, Michael says that he lost many friends in the war and by 2001 he was approaching burn-out. Subsequently he has been actively involved in the peace process, has conducted post-conflict work in Kosovo, is teaching on post-conflict issues and has undertaken many years of prison visits and works with veterans. His ultimate wish is for the reunification of Ireland.

A major theme to emerge in the walk with Michael (which also connects with the previous walks) is the idea and meaning of working through the past and how this is or is not in evidence in the visual culture of Belfast city spaces and places. Critical theorist Theodor Adorno argues for the need for 'seriously working upon the past' and not to 'close the books on the past and ... even remove it from memory' (2005: 89). Walking through Belfast city centre spaces, it appears that the traces of conflict have been expunged, yet in the Falls Road and Shankill Road, in the working class areas of New Lodge and the Markets, this past is visible in memoria in the visual culture of the murals, memorial stones and gardens. Other than visiting the Falls Road and Shankill Road to look at the murals, it is highly unlikely that a tourist or visitor would stumble across the places Michael walked. In conversation about the meaning of working through the past, Michael said:

> One of the main problems during the last round of negotiations was the British refusal to open up the past and there are people who have been killed here that still have not had a coroner's inquest forty years later, not two years later, forty years.
>
> There was a case the other day where men were tortured, and the British Government was found guilty by the European Court of Human Rights thirty years later of torturing these men and of the fourteen I think there's ten left, four have since died of natural causes and one of them said the other day I think they're just waiting until we all die and then it doesn't matter it becomes your historical footnote ... (O'Neill and Conlon, 2016: np)

In walking with Michael, it became apparent that we were literally 'walking' through the past in the present and that conflict continues to play out in the present. In response to a question asking him what walking in the city means to him, Michael talked about the need to walk fast or when not to walk and also where one could walk. 'Because it was life or death' and that 'a lot of people didn't walk because it was too dangerous, but again it's affected by the geography of the city'.

He explains:

> For instance, I can't remember the last time I was in East Belfast, I wouldn't walk in East Belfast so that's a whole quarter of the city that doesn't exist for me. I wouldn't walk in Sandy Row, I wouldn't go near the Shankill even though I worked with PUP, progressive unionist party councillors and UVF, Ulster Defence Association but I'm not sort of welcome in their territory and that's what it is. (O'Neill and Conlon, 2016: np)

Michael explains the borders of sectarianism:

> This city's divided like that river divides the city, all of it
> bar two thousand people are Loyalists on the east side of
> the river, South Belfast is mostly middle class, West Belfast
> is largely Republican and North Belfast is a minefield of
> small communities, that's where most of the walls are,
> the barriers and other things. There's a big one that runs
> up between the Falls and the Shankill. In North Belfast
> there are smaller walls and there are also what's called open
> interfaces like the West Link. This road is an open interface
> so when you drive along from the left-hand side, the side
> of the hospital, it's all Republican Nationalist, on the right
> it's all Loyalists. That road was designed to create, to do
> that, to separate the communities and Ardoyne where
> the Loyalist peace camp if you like or protest camp, it's
> an open interface. There used to be large British Army
> fortifications, they've all gone now, most of the barracks
> have gone because they don't need them anymore.
> (O'Neill and Conlon, 2016: np)

The architecture of conflict: space, place, borders and lines

Research carried out in 2011 by the Institute for Conflict Research, an
independent, not-for-profit organisation based in Belfast and funded
by the Belfast Interface Project, produced a map and comprehensive
database of the 'security barriers and defensive use of space throughout
the city, organised geographically by cluster' (Belfast Interface Project,
2011).

The report documents 99 different 'barriers' associated with
residential areas alone. These include:

- 35 barriers which are made of different styles of metal fencing;
- 23 barriers which are comprised of a mixture of a solid wall with
  metal fencing above;
- 14 examples of a mixture of fences with vegetation which acts as
  a buffer;
- 12 locations where roads have been closed to vehicles while
  allowing pedestrian access;
- eight locations where there is a wall alone; and
- seven locations where roads have gates which are closed occasionally.

These barriers are located in the following areas:

- North Belfast – defined as the area north of Crumlin Road and west of Belfast Lough;
- West Belfast – south of Crumlin Road and west of the Westlink and M1 motorway;
- the Central Area – defined as immediately adjacent to the Westlink and Inner Ring roads;
- East Belfast – east of the River Lagan and Belfast Lough;
- one barrier in South Belfast – east of the Dublin railway line, south of the city centre and west of the River Lagan.

The walks in Belfast highlighted very visibly and materially that the walls come in different shapes and sizes, as shown in Figure 6.3.

Figure 6.3: Castle Court shopping centre, car park and peace line

Image: Maggie O'Neill

So that is Castle Court, that's actually a peace line as well. The main British Army base used to be there it was a Grand Central Hotel and it was bombed, a lorry truck got them and completely flattened so they replaced it with a shopping centre and they deliberately built the car park to divide the far side of that is Nationalist, this side is for the Shankill side, so they designed, the architecture softens things but there's still walls. It looks like a car park. But it's actually a wall. (O'Neill and Conlon, 2016, np)

Walking towards New Lodge we undertook a detour. Michael says "I can't walk across this, it's too open. We'll just cut down this one." In answer to the question "and it's too open in terms of how you feel or?" Michael responds: "Yes I won't feel safe because there's lots of people have been killed along that stretch." During the walk, Michael also explained the concept of the 'architecture of conflict' and recommends a book, *Low Intensity Operations*, written by a brigadier in the British army called Frank Kitson. Kitson served in Malaya and Kenya and 'advocated that the army has to have everything working for it including the judicial system, architecture and design. So, if new houses are being built in Belfast you have one way in and one way out of a housing estate.' (O'Neill and Conlon, 2016: np) In the older streets with lots of alleyways it might take 'a couple of hundred soldiers to patrol an area like that because there are so many boltholes whereas now they have one way in, so they put an APC (Armoured personnel carrier) at the end of the street and then they have eight soldiers doing the job of two hundred' (O'Neill and Conlon, 2016: np).

The walk with Michael enabled a better sense of 'the architecture of conflict' and also the sense that in Belfast the concept of public space is a shifting concept, with spaces like the shopping centres and roads also acting as interfaces or 'walls'. The numbers of surveillance cameras were very evident too.

As you see the cameras are always in the middle of the road, everywhere you go in Belfast they're not just traffic cameras. They're linked into several commands of the police, so they can control or see what's going on. (O'Neill and Conlon, 2016, np)

Crossing North Queen Street (Figure 6.4), Michael points to a land rover.

Figure 6.4: North Queen Street

Image: Maggie O'Neill

> You see the Land Rover now? That's no bullet will go
> through that Land Rover, they evolved over a period
> of thirty years, it looks like an ordinary Land Rover but
> the sides you can see they bulk out a bit, they have like
> a one inch steel plate, they have a false ceiling at the top
> because if a throw bomb lands on the roof it used to go
> through them and kill obviously the occupants inside so
> they have a space now where so that explodes, it explodes
> between two steel plates. The windows an AK-47 won't
> go through that glass. The only thing to stop that thing
> is an RPG 7. The windows are actually gun ports.
> (O'Neill and Conlon, 2016, np)

In the New Lodge area, we came across many peace walls (see Figure
6.5) as well as murals and memorial gardens that commemorate the
dead who had lived in the area; symbols of the conflict materialised
on the buildings, houses and walls. On the side of a house there was
a mural commemorating the death of the teenage members of a local
Flute Band (Figure 6.6).

The two boys in this mural shown in Figure 6.6, Jim O'Neill and
Robert Allsopp, were 'two Fianna members, the Fianna is the junior
wing of the IRA and they were both killed, they were sixteen from a

Figure 6.5: Peace Wall

Image: Maggie O'Neill

Figure 6.6: Memorial to O'Neill and Allsopp

Image: Maggie O'Neill

Figure 6.7: New Lodge Commemoration Garden

Image: Maggie O'Neill

local band, Jim O'Neill, Memorial Flute Band' (O'Neill and Conlon, 2016, np).

> Michael describes Figure 6.7 as follows: This is the Commemoration Garden, on Easter Monday this whole community comes together and there's a couple of thousand people here and they come and lay wreaths, families lay wreaths to their dead. It was actually created about twenty years ago, we got the land from the housing executive and we tried to fix it up as best we could, but it was all local guys, local bricklayers. (O'Neill and Conlon, 2016, np)

Michael states that local people built the memorial shown in Figure 6.8: 'a welder got the railings done, the stone mason from Lurgan did the stonework for nothing but I'll just show you the names here' (O'Neill and Conlon, 2016, np).

Further examples of peace lines and walls included Hillman Street peace line, a metal gateway between a church and a row of houses, seen in Figure 6.9.

Figure 6.8: Memorial Wall

Image: Maggie O'Neill

Figure 6.9: Hillman Street Peace line

Image: Maggie O'Neill

Figure 6.10: View of the peace wall towards Duncairn Gardens

Image: Maggie O'Neill

So, we're just on the edge of the New Lodge here, this is Hillman Street, and this is the peace line here we're just about to go through. Again, these gates are closed and padlocked in the evenings, they're open during the day to let people use chemists and kids going to and from school and stuff, but this would have been a street. (O'Neill and Conlon, 2016, np)

As we approached the gate Michael describes the space between the walls, shown in Figure 6.10:

The wall is between someone's house and the church. This space has been worked out so that a petrol bomb won't go any further, so this is why it's this wide, if you've only one you can throw a petrol bomb over, so they move it to make space and you can see the houses have grilles on the windows (Figure 6.11). Even the Presbyterian Church and then further down you don't see the grilles because they're that wee bit further away and the next street going into Tigers Bay is actually sealed off, so they can't come out there and you see the anti-climb paint it means if somebody climbs up the stuff sticks to their hands. (O'Neill and Conlon, 2016, np)

Figure 6.11: Security grilles on house window

Image: Maggie O'Neill

It was both shocking and disturbing to see and experience the material presence of so many walls and gates. The dominant impression of the New Lodge area is the complex intersections between social class, poverty and the relationship with sectarianism.

> Yes, we are on the border. North Belfast is like a patchwork quilt where you have a Nationalist area, a Loyalist area, another Nationalist area, another Loyalist area and that's why the casualty rate was so high because you only had to walk across the street to kill somebody whereas in West Belfast it was sealed off by a seven mile big wall between it and the Shankill and then you had the motorway on one side so and then the British Army used to have a big barrier at the bottom at the time of the conflict they would close off so effectively they could patrol seventy odd thousand people very, very easily just by closing off the barriers and as the war went on in the 70s and the 80s and the 90s things became more sophisticated and again they started building roads where there were walls to make it look, to the outsider, as if it was normal but if you come

here at eleven o'clock at night it's definitely not normal.
(O'Neill and Conlon, 2016: np)

Landscapes of trauma, faith and security

An emerging theme was the levels of trauma in the communities and the evidence and inter-generational memories are all around; it appeared that everyone has suffered, and someone who has died in horrendous circumstances, in addition to levels of unemployment, poverty and austerity. Drug use and suicide are two social issues and problems being addressed in the area.

Walking past a block of flats Michael drew attention to the security grilles at the base of the flats and explained:

> Yes, they're all concierged, it was to try and stamp out drug dealing so we now have concierges in all the flats, so when you come in, you have to ask and know somebody in the flats, before being allowed in. (O'Neill and Conlon, 2016, np)

The play grounds are also closed here at night to stop vandals and 'like every area of deep deprivation it's common in every city and the fact it actually rose an awful lot, so did the suicide rate' (O'Neill and Conlon, 2016: np). At this time there were three suicide awareness projects in this area alone. 'It's a real crisis among young people'… the Peace Dividend as it was called never materialised in these areas, the middle class got better off but the working class didn't' (O'Neill and Conlon, 2016, np).

Walking with Michael enabled a richer insight into his biography, linked indelibly to social class, the history of republican politics, the conflict, transitional justice and the idea of the 'architecture of conflict' and its legacy. The design of public space, the car park, roads, 'peace lines' that also acted as borders and the commemoration gardens and murals that memorialised the dead, were visual reminders of sectarianism, the bloody conflict and risk played out in the neighbourhoods and city spaces.

While it is important to enable spaces for these stories to be told and heard, it is also important to reflect on the justice process and the demographic changes in Belfast too. The walk told a story about Michael's biography and is also, in part, a biography of place, of Belfast, of history in the present. The friendly exchanges on the street made possible by walking with Michael facilitated a sense of a 'convivial commons' that was undoubtedly sectarian. The material, sensory and emotional reality of the peace lines and walls, interface areas, challenged the idea of a 'successful public space' as defined by various 'opportunities to participate in communal activity'. The material and emotional impact of poverty, austerity, violence, and sectarianism in Belfast was deeply apparent in the city spaces we walked through once we left the inner city, with the erasure of references to conflict and the troubles in the very centre. The impact of the walls and barriers on the well-being of both communities across the sectarian divide was also palpable.

In summary, and as we stated earlier, it is important as sociologists and criminologists that we pay attention to the historical use and meaning of space, to the practices and cultural meanings that unfold in the use of public space, through time, including the operation of laws and state activity, to unpack the cultural meaning and use of time/space/place and its impact on well-being. Walking in both Belfast and DTES drew our attention to the use and impact of space as well as the possibilities (both utopian and productive) for 'convivial commons' and 'successful public space' opening up 'opportunities to participate in communal activity' – indeed the important relationship between resistance, sociability and community. In both communities and geographic places/spaces, there is a long way to go to achieve this. What Amin (2013) describes as 'telescopic urbanism', which focuses attention on the personal, experiential human rights and welfare-based approach to manage public space, is one possible route to engendering 'civic and political citizenship'. However, in the context of accelerating capitalism, cultures of consumption, disembedding and de-traditonalisation and the resistance to work through the past, in urban planning in both sites, this can only be articulated here as a hope.

The emergent properties of space and place – what space and place might signify and facilitate in our two sites – will not remain static, it will change. As Datta (2013) argues, it is also important to focus on the role of the law of legality. Extending this for criminologists, the operation of the criminal justice system is another important dimension to our imaginative criminological analysis of public space, place, violence and transgression; and the personal, experiential realities for marginalised groups and communities of 'working through the past'.

The transgressive acts symbolised in both the Missing Women's Memorial March and the Belfast murals and peace lines, and the operation of borders are resonant of the practices of spatial control and the impact of such practices over time in the cultural memory as well as the cultural imaginaries (evidenced through visual imageries of the march and the murals). As Seal (2014) states, to make sense of the past, 'people draw on their individual experiences and the wider social context' (p 167). Walking is a useful ethnographic method for accessing ways of knowing, meaning making and understanding of both lived experiences and cultural memory. Methodologically, our critical, historical and mobile criminological research offers a kinaesthetic, imaginative criminology for the 21st century, not only to study borders, space and place, but also to do criminology.

7

Imagining Dystopian Futures in Young Adult Fiction

Works of fiction offer great potential for doing imaginative criminology as they 'offer complex and layered social realities that can be explored criminologically and sociologically' (Frauley, 2010: 13). Fiction is vitally important to generating images and fantasies about social life and offers the possibility to create and participate in other worlds and new ways of life. This chapter explores imagined dystopias in young adult fiction as a means to think through problems of ordering, social control and repression. The novels depict undesirable worlds but in doing so offer hope for resistance and survival. The analysis of fictional worlds can demonstrate the applicability of criminological concepts and highlight issues relevant to the social world (Ruggiero, 2003; Piamonte, 2015). As such, fictional realities provide criminologists with an important pedagogical tool (Frauley, 2010). They also offer the space to think through transgression, plurality and power in a way that is more open and alive to multiplicity than criminology usually permits.

While fictional realities in films and television programmes have received attention, few criminologists have explored literature. Piamonte (2015) argues that novels enable creative criminological sense making about important social themes, such as her examination of the portrayal of violence and racism in Wright's (1940) *Native Son*. Ruggiero (2015) explores the depiction of crimes of the powerful in the novels of Balzac, the sociological analyses of imprisonment that can be derived from Victor Hugo and Octave Mirbeau (Ruggiero, 2012) and the different aspects of war portrayed by Stendhal and Tolstoy (Ruggiero, 2018). Page and Goodman (2018) analyse how Edward Bunker's novels on prison life further understanding of the subjective experience of incarceration.

Previous criminological analyses of novels demonstrate their significance for imaginative criminology but have largely been restricted to 'canonical' literature, rather than fiction that intersects with popular culture. They are also concerned predominantly with literary realism. This chapter departs from this focus to consider how mass market dystopian fiction for young adults facilitates the imagining of undesirable futures and reflection on social injustices in the present. Young adult (YA) fiction typically adopts a pedagogical role in terms of expanding readers' understanding of themselves and the world (Bull, 2012). While this can be didactic, it is subversive in placing young people at the centre of narratives in which adults are peripheral, absent and/or in opposition to the protagonists (Hintz and Ostry, 2003). YA fiction frequently highlights issues of social inequality and social injustice and can aid young people in developing critical analyses of how society is classed, gendered and raced (Hintz and Ostry, 2003; Taber et al, 2013). This development of critical literacy can contribute to inspiring transformative knowledge and practice (Simmons, 2012; Morton and Lounsbury, 2015). Fiction can open up the space for the development of a radical democratic imaginary.

Dystopian and post-apocalyptic fiction has been at the forefront of publishing for young adults since the mid 2000s although the trend connects to and draws on well-established conventions of the genre (Pharr and Clark, 2012; Basu et al, 2013). Series such as *Uglies*, *The Hunger Games*, *The Maze Runner* and *Divergent* have been hugely successful commercially, both as novels and in the case of the latter three, as film franchises. This popularity can be attributed to their propensity for dealing with 'pressing global concerns' such as free will and self-determination, environmental destruction, questions of identity and subjectivity, and the boundaries between technology and the self (Basu et al, 2013: 1). Dystopian societies are depicted as worse than those of our present but also reimagine aspects of the present in the future (Pharr and Clark, 2012; Basu et al, 2013). This is the critical role of dystopia: to both critique the current world but also to leave space for hope and change, and pathways to better futures (Morrissey, 2013; Elliot, 2015).

The heroes of contemporary dystopian YA fiction are typically engaged in fighting totalitarian governments in societies in which adults either exercise repressive power or are the ineffectual or indoctrinated victims of these regimes (Pharr and Clark, 2012; Morton and Lounsbury, 2015). As such, power is a key theme (Pulliam, 2014; Morton and Lounsbury, 2015). Adolescence marks the point at which the protagonist must undergo some form of rite of passage, initiation or trial, often preceding integration into 'their society's controlling framework' (Green-Barteet, 2014: 34). Conformity and rebellion are therefore strong themes, as are loss of innocence and awakening to the true nature of society (Basu et al, 2013). The protagonists are frequently exceptional individuals who come of age – either as self-governing subjects or recuperated objects of the regime (Broad, 2013; Green-Barteet, 2014; Morton and Lounsbury, 2015).

This chapter explores analysis of contemporary dystopian YA fiction as a way of doing imaginative criminology. It considers four novels – *The Hunger Games* (Collins, 2008), *The Maze Runner* (Dashner, 2009), *Divergent* (Roth, 2011) and *Red Rising* (Brown, 2014) – all of which are the first instalment in a trilogy. The first three have been adapted into films (and *Red Rising* is in development) but the discussion will focus on the books. These novels depict imagined futures and/or alternative societies and therefore present fictional geographies that exist solely within the imagination. As such, they employ images and symbols to create representational space (Lefebvre, 1991). In doing so, all four novels engage with virtual reality and portray spaces that do not have a physical surface (Warf and Arias, 2009). The following analysis examines four recurrent themes: spectacle, surveillance and control; hyperreality/virtual reality; memory and suppressed history; and hierarchy, segregation and difference. Before addressing these, the content of each book is briefly outlined.

The Hunger Games: set in Panem, a post-apocalyptic United States. The population either lives a comfortable life in the Capitol or a hard one in the surrounding Districts. Each year, two adolescents – known as tributes – from each District are selected to take part in the Hunger Games, a televised spectacle that takes place in an arena and involves a fight for survival against the other tributes and the trials and tests set by the Games' makers. The final remaining tribute is the winner. Protagonist Katniss Everdeen of District 12 volunteers to take her younger sister's place in the Games. She and fellow tribute from her District Peeta Mellark manage to survive and unprecedentedly both emerge as winners after they threaten to kill themselves by swallowing poisoned berries rather than sacrifice each other.

The Maze Runner: protagonist Thomas awakes in a strange place, the Glade, an environment populated by teenage boys who have organised themselves into a functioning and orderly community. He has no memory of his previous life. The Glade is attached to a maze, which the boys believe holds the solution to their escape and which they attempt to map. Strange events start to occur once Teresa, the first girl, arrives. Once Thomas and some of the others manage to leave the Glade, they learn millions of deaths were caused by a series of sun flares, which precipitated a deadly virus called The Flare. Assessed to be of high aptitude, the boys were being tested to discover their suitability for helping to find how to combat the virus. The Gladers are rescued from the scientists conducting the experiment by what appears to be a rebel group, but the epilogue reveals this is another stage of the simulated trial.

Divergent: the setting is post-apocalyptic Chicago, which operates as a city state based on a population divided into four factions: Abnegation, Amity, Erudite and Dauntless. Membership of the factions accords with character and values, and each faction is responsible for different aspects of running the city. Protagonist Tris Prior has grown up in Abnegation, which is based on values of selflessness and administers the city's government. At 16, individuals undergo a test that generates an assessment of which faction they are most suited for and participate in a ceremony called The Choosing, in which they select a faction. Tris discovers that she is divergent; she has the characteristics of more than one faction but is told to hide her divergence. At The Choosing she selects Dauntless, which is based on courage, and leaves her previous life and family. During her period of initiation, she realises that the Erudite faction (based on intelligence) has devised a plot to overthrow the Abnegation government by using a serum to control the Dauntless through use of simulation, turning them into a mindless army. As a Divergent, Tris is able to resist simulations and is able to orchestrate the defeat of Erudite's plan.

Red Rising: the action takes place in a distant future in which humans have colonised other planets. Social status is determined through a genetically engineered caste system based on colour, in which Reds are at the bottom and Golds are at the top. Protagonist Darrow is a Red, who works as a 'hell diver' in the mines on Mars and lives underground. The Reds are supposedly working to terraform the planet for human inhabitants. After being sentenced to death Darrow is rescued by a resistance group, the Sons of Ares, and learns that Mars has in fact been inhabited for centuries and is technologically advanced. The Sons of Ares have him physically and neurologically remodelled into a Gold so that he can infiltrate Gold society. Darrow gains admission to the Golds' Institute where he is selected to progress to The Passage, where contenders are divided into four Houses, each with a fortress which they must defend while trying to capture the others. Performing well means gaining sponsorship and a successful future career. Darrow manages to triumph and chooses the ruler of Mars Augustus as his patron in order to work towards overthrowing the Gold elite.

Spectacle, surveillance and control

Contemporary YA dystopian fiction portrays heavily controlled and surveilled societies in which spectacle is a key means of subduing and entertaining the population. Control is exerted by shadowy non-democratic or totalitarian governments or, in the case of *The Maze Runner*, by unknown forces (later revealed to be part of a scientific experiment). Pulliam (2014) notes that *The Hunger Games'* Panem is a hybrid of a sovereign society and a disciplinary society. The televised spectacle of the Games and the use of public corporal punishment display the Capitol's power and the various Districts are heavily policed by 'peacekeepers' who can mete out punishment. Districts are separated from one another by geographical region but also bounded by barbed wire and electrified fences in an effort to reduce the fomenting of rebellion (Wezner, 2012). The Capitol's power is underwritten and secured via spatial segregation. Preparation for the Games demonstrates how the tributes must learn to discipline themselves to be palatable for the audience located in the Capitol in terms of dress, appearance and demeanour.

The Hunger Games are the foremost demonstration of the Capitol's sovereign power and are held both as a legacy punishment for an earlier rebellion from the Districts and as spectacular entertainment. Witnessing them is compulsory. The 24 tributes must fight to the death and the winner and their family are financially secure for life – with the caveat that they must help to train future tributes. The Games are brutal and violent but as television they also entail playing a part and being aware of the preferences of the audience. Attracting sponsors means that useful gifts will be sent to the arena. To this end, Katniss and Peeta enact a developing romance. The Games' participants are under constant surveillance and all of their actions are recorded. The arena is panoptically structured, radiating out from a central 'cornucopia' from which the Games commence (Wezner, 2012). Muller (2012) identifies the Games as drawing on a gladiatorial paradigm of festive spectacle, with the naming of the participants as 'tributes' recalling the Roman practice of exacting monetary tributes from the populace as a sign of obedience. The country's name – Panem – also has the Roman resonance of 'Panem et Circenses': control based on the provision of food and entertainment.

References to ancient Greece and Rome are significant in *Red Rising*, in which the ArchGovernor of Mars is named Nero Augustus and other elite families bear names such as Bellona. The novel opens with the protagonist Darrow's account of his father's public hanging. He explains that executions on Mars are televised and that the bodies of the condemned remain on the scaffold as the Reds are not allowed to bury their dead. The men work in the mines from aged 13, their lives governed by strict rules enforced through terror and hard work. Spatially, the Reds live in a panopticon; their townships surround a central Common. Each one has a 'holoCan' – a square box that projects propaganda images from the ruling Society on each of its screens and is never turned off. This tells the Reds that they are working to terraform Mars for human habitation and shows above ground as a wasteland. The holoCan also broadcasts news of terrorist attacks by the rebel Sons of Ares group.

Like Panem, the regime portrayed in *Red Rising* fuses sovereign and disciplinary power, enacted through spatial organisation. More food and small luxuries for the whole town can be gained by winning the Laurel for mining the greatest volume of helium-3. However, the contest is rigged, favouring one town in particular and meaning that Darrow never wins. Darrow and his wife Eo break the rules and venture above ground by climbing through a grate into a forest where they see sky, vegetation and animal life for the first time. As punishment, they are publicly whipped on the Common, which they see being simultaneously broadcast on the holoCan. Eo sings a protest song in defiance and is immediately hanged; Darrow is subsequently hanged for taking her body down from the gallows but is saved by the Sons of Ares.

The role of spectacle is more ambiguous in *The Maze Runner* as the boys who live in the Glade do not know who is watching them or to what end, but they know that they are subject to the control of the Creators who programme the Maze. Thomas realises that the ubiquitous mechanical beetle blades record life in the Glade. The boys have established an orderly society in which they take on different work-based roles such as cooking, cleaning or growing food – or they are 'Runners' who attempt to fathom the secret of the Maze. They have a system of rules, enforce minor punishments for their infraction, and have maintained their society for two years with new boys arriving each month. The boys' disciplined, collaborative conduct is the opposite of the social breakdown depicted in *Lord of the Flies* (Golding, 1954). The imperative to navigate the Maze binds them in a shared purpose and illustrates the effectiveness of disciplinary power and the manipulation of space.

Divergent's post-apocalyptic Chicago is a city-state with no connections to other states or territories. It is not a democracy but neither is it obviously authoritarian. The city is spatially divided by faction, with the separation of communities being an important mechanism of social control (Roszak, 2016). Most of the city's residents have very little spatial mobility; only one faction, the Dauntless, rides the former L train system, enabling faster movement across the urban landscape. Tris's description of Abnegation is of a safe and orderly community against which she chafes. Abnegation must think of others before themselves and are dedicated to public works. Their grey, uniform houses evoke the Communist societies of mid 20th-century Eastern Europe and the Soviet Union – indicating that safety and order come at a price.

Tris's metamorphosis into a member of Dauntless involves changing her appearance, behaviour and manner of social interaction. Self-policing of these elements is highly important in order to fit in and underlines how Tris's world is one based on a pervasive sense of surveillance, even where it is not enacted technologically. Whereas the Abnegation are faceless civil servants, the Dauntless are responsible for the city's security and patrol its borders, an indication that it also employs harder forms of power to protect its existence.

Hyperreality/virtual reality

All four of the novels contain significant elements of virtual reality, simulated experiences and the hyperreal, particularly in relation to drawing on computer games for inspiration. Hyperreality is the management and manipulation of simulations that are indistinguishable from reality (Baudrillard, 1991). The arena in *The Hunger Games* is a simulation – it is manipulated by the Games makers who design the landscape and populate it with flora and fauna and can visit trials and disasters on the tributes to raise the drama and entertainment value for the audience (Muller, 2012). They do this completely amorally; it is a fight to the death and inflicting pain and suffering is integral to the gladiatorial contest. The arena becomes a tourist attraction after the Games have finished, mirroring Disneyland and evoking Baudrillard's (1993) concept of the hyperreal (Day, 2012; Tan, 2013). The Games are primarily a satire on contests familiar from reality television, where participants are pitted against one another and there can be only one winner. As tributes meet their deaths through murder and misadventure their images and District number are beamed to the arena and the wider audience.

Collins (2008) emphasises the cruelty at the centre of contests waged for entertainment and highlights the emotional and moral distance of the audience. Day (2012: 167) argues that *The Hunger Games* draws inspiration from *The Running Man* and *Battle Royale* in depicting 'the role of television as repressive' and a tool of distraction. In *The Running Man* (Bachman/King, 1982) the poor and desperate participate in the government-controlled Games Network's brutal game shows, risking their health and their lives for the slim chance of winning cash rewards.

Ben, the protagonist, signs up for The Running Man, which involves the chance to win a hundred dollars for each hour he can avoid being hunted down by the show's 'stalkers' or turned in by the public. The film adaptation (Glaser, 1987) places the action in an arena and makes the contestants convicted criminals. The randomly selected secondary school students in *Battle Royale* (Takami, 1999) are forced to participate in a government programme where they are transported to a remote location and must fight to the death leaving one winner. The game has 'an entertainment function' as well as being a means of terrifying the population (Day, 2012: 171).

The perpetration of warfare and violence in a simulated environment also draws on the modality of computer games and it is this type of virtual reality that is most prominently emulated in YA dystopian fiction. *Divergent*'s Tris undergoes repeated simulations, brought on by a serum, in which she must face her fears as part of her training for entry into the Dauntless faction. Subjection to these scenarios is reminiscent of *1984*'s (Orwell, 1949) Room 101 and Alex's aversion therapy in *A Clockwork Orange* (Burgess, 1962), but their format reflects the role play of a computer game. As a 'divergent', Tris is able to perceive that the simulations are not real and can therefore redirect them. The heroism of Tris and fellow divergent Tobias results from their ability to resist the blurring of reality and simulation, which enables them to defeat the Erudite.

The computer game modality is central to both *Red Rising* and *The Maze Runner*. The bulk of *Red Rising* depicts Darrow's experience of The Passage, the ordeal that helps to determine the young Golds' futures. The events are action based and evoke both ancient mythology and, in keeping with the computer game inspiration, a fantasy-style medieval war game. The contest is ultimately controlled and manipulated by the Proctors, who oversee The Passage and who have been bribed by ArchGovernor Augustus. Although taking place in a medieval landscape of fortresses and packs of wolves, Proctors can introduce elements such as gravity boots, invisibility cloaks and protective force fields that evoke simulation.

The Maze Runner most fully utilises a computer game modality and does so to question the nature of reality. Thomas awakes in The Glade and, like the player of a game, needs to work out what kind of world and society he is in. As new arrivals must, he tries out different work-based tasks to find his niche and how he can contribute to life in the Glade. He feels an irresistible urge to become a Runner, one of the boys who enter the Maze when its doors open each day in an effort to map out its shifting walls and floors. When they return before the

Glade is sealed for the night, each runner draws maps of his particular section. In this way, the boys attempt to solve the labyrinth. While in the Maze they must avoid the Grievers, horrific creatures with lethal stings that live in the Maze. This shifting puzzle, which has hidden dangers, is clearly influenced by computer games. The boys are aware that they live in a reality they do not control; that it is a simulation becomes increasingly clear as the usual pattern of events is disturbed. After Teresa's arrival, the doors to the Maze stay open, allowing the Grievers into the Glade, and the sun goes out.

Memory and suppressed history

The hyperreal and virtual reality elements of these dystopian novels are intimately connected to the theme of loss of collective memory and suppressed history. In *The Hunger Games* and *Divergent*, some kind of cataclysm in the past has led to a period of war and conflict, followed by the establishment of the regimes under which Katniss and Tris live. Both books are set in societies which have developed in what was previously the United States. The nature of these disastrous events is not known and in these first instalments of the respective trilogies, the main characters show no curiosity about the history of their societies or how they came to be as they are.

The Hunger Games are Panem's history; there are recordings of the Games stretching back over more than 70 years, which are the only events to be preserved in collective memory in this way (Muller, 2012). The recordings are an unreliable archive that serves the needs of the Capitol. During the Games, Katniss covers the body of Rue, a 12-year-old tribute who reminds her of her younger sister, with flowers. Afterwards, she sees that this act was edited from the broadcast recording. As Tan (2013) argues, there is no world outside Panem. Its residents' cultural memory and history are centred on the Games and controlled by the Capitol. Morton and Lounsbury (2015: 60) state that *The Hunger Games* trilogy 'highlights the importance of knowledge of the past as a catalyst to bring about political and ideological renewal'. This resonates with the critical recovery of history to cultivate democracy advocated by critical theory (O'Neill, 2011).

The post-apocalyptic Chicago of *Divergent* is similarly isolated from a larger context. It is identifiable to the reader through references to street names, landmarks such as the Hancock Building and the L Train system ridden by the Dauntless. What was formerly Lake Michigan has become a huge marsh. How the city came to be segregated into sections and fenced off as its own separate society is therefore a question that occurs to the reader, even if in *Divergent* it does not occur to Tris. The subsequent two books of the trilogy portray Tris's discovery of the city's history as part of a government-approved experiment on divergents, which entailed sequestering it from the rest of the country. This historical knowledge is an important spur to Tris's rebellious actions (Morton and Lounsbury, 2015).

Suppression of truth about the past is fundamental to the control of the Reds in *Red Rising* as they are unaware that Mars has been settled for centuries. Labouring in the mines and living underground means that their knowledge of anything else is restricted to what is screened on the holoCans and related to them by visiting officials. The Reds have developed their own cultural memory through song and tradition but have done so without knowing their true position. They believe that they are pioneers working for the noble cause of making Mars fit for habitation, rather than exploited dupes.

The role of the uncertainty and instability of memory is most powerfully explored in *The Maze Runner*. Thomas has a strong sense of a previous life about which he can remember nothing. As Elliot (2015) notes, he has procedural memory in the sense of knowing how to perform tasks and being able to identify what things are but lacks personal history. Thomas's lost memory is a lost history; he only has the present of the Glade through which to develop a sense of self. He becomes convinced that both the Glade and the Maze are familiar and the strange turn of events in the Glade appears to have been triggered by his arrival. Learning about his past and discovering what the Maze is for rather than just trying to map it propel him into action (Morton and Lounsbury, 2015).

First-person narration by a protagonist who does not know who he is is an effective and disturbing device. Although the protagonists of the other three books are ignorant or deceived about the societies in which they live, they have personal history. Coupled with the simulated reality of the Glade and the Maze, Thomas's unmooring from his personal memory raises questions about the nature of reality and existence. Elliot (2015) reads *The Maze Runner* as trauma narrative in which memory loss, skewed temporality and lack of communication are significant. Rather than portraying trauma, the narrative performs trauma through depiction of an individual who enters a new world and must remake his life. The Maze, which is ever changing and non-linear, symbolises the complexity of trauma and the desire of those who experience it to derive meaning from it.

The Gladers have a 'grief serum' that they can administer to Runners who get stung by a Griever. This saves their lives but induces a process known as the Changing, during which some of their memories return with haunting effects. Elliot (2015) argues that the Grievers embody the horror of grief and the Changing the process of confronting trauma. The boys who have undergone the Changing emerge disturbed and in some cases psychotic. They also raise the possibility that the world outside the Glade is not worth returning to. Thomas intentionally gets stung in an effort to recover some of his memories and realises that he played a role in helping to design the Maze and that he has links with the mysterious World in Catastrophe: Killzone Experiment Department (WICKED), which appears to control the Glade.

Hierarchy, segregation and difference

The connections between difference, hierarchy, segregation and power are a strong theme of YA dystopian literature. *The Hunger Games*, *Red Rising* and *Divergent* all depict societies that are unequal and divided by wealth and status. Life in Panem's Districts is hard and marked by deprivation and hunger to the point of starvation. The regime's subjects labour to ensure the material comfort of the residents of the Capitol, who eat lavish meals and wear fashionable clothes, and are seemingly oblivious to the suffering of those in the Districts. This is clearly intended to mirror present-day global inequalities between the Global North and South but also those within the United States.

The situating of Katniss's home of District 12 in Appalachia underlines these resonances. Badagliacco and Ruiz (2006: 215) argue that echoes of early 20th-century eugenics persist 'today in many of the stereotypes of Appalachian Kentucky poor, rural families' and that 'debasing stereotypes that suggest poverty, ignorance, stupidity and immorality abound'. Scott (2009: 805) identifies the powerful binary cultural representation of Appalachians as simple 'patriotic ideal citizens' and 'backwoods horrors'. Appalachia is both romanticised and associated with derogatory 'white trash' stereotypes. The discussion generated by Vance's (2016) *Hillbilly Elegy* demonstrates how the cultural resonance of Appalachia and white rural poverty has gained renewed strength since the election of Donald Trump, when media attention focused on the 'white working class' voters who supposedly sealed his victory (see Rothman, 2016; Senior, 2016).

Unlike the other three novels explored in this chapter, *Red Rising* does not portray society transformed by a cataclysm, but rather human society several centuries in the future. Colour entirely determines placement in the social scale. Reds like Darrow are at the bottom, performing hard labour and menial jobs, Golds constitute an aristocratic ruling elite. In between are a host of colour-based castes such as Coppers, who are bureaucrats, and Oranges, who are technicians. After Darrow is rescued from hanging by the Sons of Ares they take him to Mickey, a 'Carver', who transforms him into a Gold through neural surgery and physical remodelling. Mickey explains of the Golds 'It took generations of eugenics and biological tampering to make them. Forced Darwinism' (Brown, 2014).

Red Rising imagines a dystopia based on power differences established and held in place through genetically engineering humans but it also suggests that this system is not impermeable. For Darrow to become a Gold he must learn their culture and comportment in addition to his physical transformation; these elements are as much a part of being Gold as genetic lineage. It also becomes clear that Darrow's strength, dexterity and endurance developed through 'hell diving' in the mines make him a formidable opponent in The Passage, and that he possesses skills the Golds do not. His realisation that rival Titus is also a Red who has managed to infiltrate the Institute highlights that Colour identity is porous rather than fixed.

The city's factionless in *Divergent* are marginalised in terms of power, influence, status and material security. Like the residents of Panem's Districts and the Reds in Brown's trilogy they serve the needs of others. The arrangement of the city into factions is designed to prevent conflict and is seemingly benign. However, it is partly kept in place by the threat of exile. Those who fail to perform adequately in their chosen faction's initiation are doomed to abjection. They live in the city's slums and carry out unskilled and semi-skilled work. The factionless appear to be an underclass who live without the protection of the city's infrastructure – they merely work to maintain it.

All four novels imagine unequal and stratified societies that appear to be post capitalist. Large powerful corporations are not a feature of the exercise of power and control, unlike, for example, the private security company CorpSecorps in *Oryx and Crake* (Atwood, 2003). Material inequality and hierarchy are portrayed as unjust but there is no connection drawn between the capitalist present and the cataclysms and inequalities of the future. An example of this is the *Lazarus* comics, which depict the mid 21st-century world as clearly post capitalist (Rucka et al, 2013-ongoing). It is divided into blocs under the control of a small group of wealthy families, whose ascent to power derived from their successful business ventures in the 20th century.

In addition to signalling class inequality, Roszak (2016) argues that YA dystopian fiction draws attention to race by depicting hierarchical or segregated societies, but without directly representing it. She describes this as 'echoing without naming' (p 61). *Divergent* is a case in point. The segregation of the city into different factions that coexist but do not intermix echoes racial segregation but the factions are not based on race or ethnicity. The setting of post-apocalyptic Chicago amplifies the echoes of racial inequality, as the city has a well-known history of residential division along ethnic and racial lines (see Burgess, 1928). This echoing without naming makes the symbolism of the factions flexible; they can be interpreted as standing for multiple hierarchies and differences. However, it also means that issues of racial and ethnic injustice are not tackled overtly (Roszak, 2016). Basu (2013) interprets *Divergent* as ultimately reinforcing the idea that people have fixed traits, highlighting the conservatism of much YA dystopian fiction. Roszak (2016) counters that taken as a whole, the trilogy advocates the benefits of cultural hybridity but is characteristic of the genre's lack of explicit attention to race.

The Hunger Games and *Red Rising* both engage in echoing racial injustice without naming it through depicting or alluding to systems of slavery. Couzelis (2013) notes that Rue and Thresh, the tributes from District 11, are the only characters in *The Hunger Games* to be identified in terms of race; their physical description indicates that they are African-American. Rue's account of life in District 11, the agricultural district, implies it is based on slavery. Unlike in District 12, public whipping is frequent and routine, rather than occasional. Her use of song as a form of communication evokes the significance of 19th-century slave songs to African-American expression and survival (see Capuano, 2003). Couzelis (2013) is critical of this echoing without naming of racial injustice as enabling narrative silence on race, making it unimportant. She emphasises in particular that the place of Rue and Thresh in the narrative is to help the character development of Katniss, a white girl, rather than to explore their agency or history.

In *Red Rising*, Darrow understands that the lowReds were enslaved when he learns about how they have been deceived and also that there is a slightly higher caste, the highReds, who do menial work but live above ground. Similarly to *The Hunger Games*, the importance of song to the lowReds as both a form of resistance and to express cultural experiences evokes African-American slave history. The 'Darwinism' of the social system also has strong racial connotations, especially as it is colour that marks the place of individuals in the social order. However, like *Divergent* and *The Hunger Games*, *Red Rising* does not deal head on with race issues analogous to the present day. The system of colours has been created through genetic engineering over centuries so we can infer this is a different racial system, unrelated to the one of the present and more biologically determined. This approach is in keeping with Couzelis's (2013) point about the reluctance of YA dystopian fiction to address race in a way that is socially and culturally resonant.

In *The Hunger Games*, *Divergent* and *Red Rising* the young people's contests and rites of passage are not divided along gender lines. Girls and boys compete against one another, including in terms of combat. Districts must each provide a girl and a boy to participate in *The Hunger Games* but once in the arena they are all equally involved in a fight to the death. In this sense, the importance of gender is downplayed although the preparation for the Games highlights the significance of embodied performances of femininity and masculinity to the audience. Katniss is made over by her stylists, which includes attention to hair, make up and dress, as well as extensive depilation. In the phase before the Games, the girl tributes must appear as 'stereotypical feminine beauties' (Pulliam, 2014: 176). Katniss is able to be disciplined in terms of adopting an appearance consistent with emphasised femininity but remains more comfortable in shirts and trousers.

Before the Games, Katniss has never performed this kind of hyperfemininity as she has been focused on the need to survive, and to ensure the survival of her mother and sister. Pulliam (2014) argues that Katniss is androgynous, exhibiting masculine and feminine qualities. She is a proficient hunter, a fierce combatant and a shrewd tactician in battle. Adopting the role of 'star crossed lover' for the Games does not come easily as she is not emotionally demonstrative and must consciously remind herself to show affection for Peeta – who is portrayed as more emotionally intelligent than Katniss. At the same time, she is motivated to act predominantly through her care for others. Her father's death left her mother immobilised by grief and Katniss effectively became mother to her younger sister, Prim. In the arena of the Games she adopts a similar role in relation to Rue and also nurses Peeta back to health when he is severely injured.

Tris Prior is similarly androgynous and exhibits less conventional femininity than Katniss in her rejection of a life of self-sacrifice in Abnegation for one of adventure in Dauntless. Faction is so important to the performance of identity that it governs dress and appearance more than gender does. Katniss Everdeen learned her hunting skills from her father; Tris discovers that her Dauntless characteristics come from her mother. There is less potential for gender crossing in *Red Rising* and *The Maze Runner* as they feature active male protagonists.

Darrow's involvement with the Sons of Ares is precipitated by the rebellion of Eo, his wife, who is also more clear-sighted than he is about the Reds' life as one of exploitation, but the focus of the narrative is the making of Darrow as a warrior and leader. The homosocial world of the Glade in *The Maze Runner* is disrupted by the arrival of Teresa, the first girl, who tells the boys that the Ending will be triggered. The book is mainly devoted to the interactions between the boys and the society that they have created in the Glade, with femininity figured as a destructive force.

As coming-of-age narratives, all four novels explore the burgeoning sexuality of their protagonists as a constituent element of their journeys to maturity. They do so within the confines of heteronormativity, highlighting Basu et al's (2013: 8) point that YA dystopian fiction rarely depicts queer relationships and is reluctant to 'subvert dominant mores' in relation to sexuality. Queerness is absent from *The Hunger Games*, *Divergent* and *The Maze Runner*, in which the protagonists experience developing heterosexual attraction. The place and meaning of desire, sex and subjectivity beyond heterosexuality in the societies portrayed is not addressed. Queerness in *Red Rising* is represented by the Pinks, sexual servants who have been bred to be desirable and to give pleasure to higher colours. As such, the Pinks are portrayed as debased and without agency although the character of Matteo, a Pink who is a member of the Sons of Ares and instructs Darrow in Gold manners and culture, shows that Pinks, like the Reds, are capable of developing political consciousness and of rebelling.

The absence and marginalisation of queerness in these narratives relates to the lack of any radical departure from gender norms. Although young women are depicted as able to successfully engage in combat as warriors, there is no troubling of the division of gender into female and male. None of the characters are gender fluid and despite the portrayals of genetic and bodily modification, there is no mention of gender transition. The lack of speculation about future sexualities in these novels can be attributed to their commercial priorities. Marketed to be bestsellers and adapted or optioned as Hollywood films, they avoid the potential contentiousness of depicting queer sexualities and non-binary gender identities. It could be argued that dystopias by definition would not be accepting of diverse genders and sexualities but the texts explored in this chapter do not examine how this would be policed and controlled if this were the case, unlike, for example, the recent TV adaptation of *The Handmaid's Tale* (2017; 2018). Rather, there is a narrative silence.

Conclusion

Young adult dystopian fiction offers fertile ground for imaginative criminology in portraying post-capitalist, post-democratic societies. Conceptualising the future is a means of critiquing the present but also of sounding a warning about the possible consequences of our current social, political and economic trajectories. In this sense, it assists with 'resisting social and political decay' (Ruggiero, 2018: 1). Bestselling fiction is an 'important area of culture in capitalist societies' and therefore an important source of cultural sense making (Fiske, 2010: 85). To become popular, texts are relevant to and resonate with everyday life and our current condition (Fiske, 2010). This relevance and resonance offers substantial possibilities for being critical of the misuse of power and of social injustice. Contemporary concerns about the health of democracy in countries such as Hungary, Poland, Turkey and crucially the United States have increased the relevance and resonance of dystopian fiction.

Capitalist imperatives do appear to limit the range and extent of this critique in terms of the four selected novels – they have little to say about capitalism itself, avoid depicting queerness or non-binary gender and only portray racial inequality obliquely. This is not to argue that they could not be read in alternative ways but the themes of surveillance and hyperreality are much stronger and are more fully embedded in the narrative. The most subversive theme in these texts is the manipulation of history and collective memory as it invites scepticism about how history is told and how memory is constructed, while emphasising the need for memory and the recovery of history as the basis for resistance. This chimes with many of our previous examples in this book and is consistent with the project of critical theory (see O'Neill, 2011).

The pedagogical uses of YA dystopian fiction include the potential, through storytelling, to critique the misuse of power in order to foster democracy. As Page and Goodman (2018) argue, fiction can create scenarios that researchers cannot observe. For criminologists, YA dystopian fiction is a cultural resource with which to envision the future and to highlight the necessity for change – while also retaining hope. Like the ghost stories we discussed in Chapter 4, it offers the possibility for transcending realism and fully engaging the imagination. Creating a radical democratic imaginary involves thinking beyond the here-and-now and, where necessary, thinking beyond the currently possible.

8

Conclusion

Our aim in this book has been to argue for and do imaginative criminology. Through a range of contrasting and complementary examples, we have shown the rich analysis that emerges from the use of creative methodologies and the examination of biographical and fictive sources. In this concluding chapter, we return to the notion of the criminological imagination and how it might be expanded. We reflect on our main findings and arguments, and our theoretical contributions. We also highlight certain key areas for further development in criminology, in terms of both empirical and conceptual work.

There are three main prongs to the sociological imagination: attention to the social structure; attention to place in history; and attention to the biographical and experiential (Wright Mills, 1959; Frauley, 2015b; O'Neill et al, 2015). Imaginative criminology engages with all three. Our methodological toolbox enables deep engagement with the biographical and experiential. The oral history interviews utilised with Indigenous Australians removed to children's homes in Chapter 2 and women who spent time in Magdalene laundries in Chapter 3 are of course deeply biographical and shed light on the lived experience of these institutions. They unlock personal memories and illustrate how memory involves mediation between past and present, personal identity and past experience and individual and collective memories (Thomson, 2007; Seal, 2014). Publicly accessible online archives of oral history testimonies form part of cultural memory. Similarly, memoir and documentaries are sources involving the articulation of lived experience and memory in order to tell stories about the social world (Roberts, 2015).

Creative writing is another way to express personal biography and experience, as is evocatively demonstrated by the poems written by prisoners in Chapter 4. These communicate the subjective experience of incarceration and how state power enacted through punishment is felt and lived by individuals. Unlike oral history testimony, creative writing enables the writer to exceed their own story and to imagine other lives and contexts. The ghost stories also discussed in Chapter 4 offer trenchant examples of this, in which themes of haunting and trauma predominate. Creative methodologies such as writing present criminologists with the possibility of transcending positivist conceptions of truth and objectivity and enabling subjective expression. This is a different kind of 'data' from that which criminologists usually collect, even when they use qualitative methods. It facilitates engagement with aspects of experience such as affective states and understandings of the relationship between self and others, past and present, the individual and the collective.

Walking methodologies also allow the recovery of personal biography and facilitate storytelling, as the examples in Chapters 4, 5 and 6 illustrate (see also O'Neill and Roberts 2019). This involves relating individual biography as demonstrated by the walks Maggie O'Neill did with John Perivolaris in Chios and Michael Conlon in Belfast. However, as the accounts of these walks exemplify, the embodied experience of moving through space is also a means to tell the multiple stories of different places, including their traumatic pasts and presents. In Chios this involved encountering refugee camps and the shaping of the local by the global, and in Belfast the history of the Troubles and ongoing sectarian and class-based divisions. The Durham ghost walk entailed landmarks associated with crime and punishment, highlighting their presence in the physical landscape but also evoking how each town and city is a palimpsest superimposed on sites of historical punishments such as public hanging. Walking – or marching – is also a well-established form of social protest, as explored in relation to Vancouver's Women's Memorial March in Chapter 6. This march raises cultural visibility of the deaths of women from the Downtown Eastside (DTES) through poverty and violence and instantiates them in cultural memory.

Analysis of representations in fictive sources has been another important strand of our imaginative criminological methodology. Feature films and novels tell stories that 'bridge the gap between the inner life of human actors and the historical and social setting in which they find themselves' (Young, 2011: 2). The feature films discussed in Chapters 2 and 3 are fictional versions of 'real' stories, which they bring to wide national and international audiences. For criminologists, analysing these representations develops an understanding of how they help to form cultural memory and also how fictional sources are 'feeling forms' that engage audiences with the experiences of marginalised people (O'Neill, 2001). The dystopian novels explored in Chapter 7 create different or alternative worlds, which are inevitably also a portrait of our own. They activate another aspect of the sociological imagination – speculation (Wright Mills, 1959; Frauley, 2015b) – and enable criminologists to think through future trajectories of repressive power and social division.

As this discussion of the methodologies and forms of imaginative criminology makes clear, imaginative criminology involves the linking of the biographical and experiential to both wider social structures and its place in history. Social inequalities of race, ethnicity, gender, citizenship and class are relevant across all of our examples. Individual stories and biographies can be situated in relation to social position, which is shaped by social structures. Chapters 2 and 3 engage with histories of confinement in Australia and Ireland, and the ways in which confinement was utilised by the state to fix in place white and patriarchal privilege. These examples evince how the past resonates in the present, and continues to be lived and imagined in the present. The meeting of histories in the physical landscape is significant to the walks recounted in Chapters 4, 5 and 6, and legacies of colonial domination and conflict shape the current experiences of people in refugees in camps in southern Europe and living in the post-conflict landscape of Belfast.

In doing imaginative criminology, we paid attention to the significance of different imaginaries. The dominant social imaginary entails imagining the boundaries of collectives and communities; it plays a role in the exclusion of certain individuals and groups. However, the imaginary is constituted creatively through images, stories and fantasy and this creativity is a means for envisioning justice and better worlds. Counter, alternative and subaltern imaginaries proliferate. Across the chapters, we have highlighted how social control restricts the imaginary domain of individuals but also how this domain can be nurtured in hostile surroundings, preserving a sense of self and dignified self-presentation.

Transgression, ordering and space

Our various examples explored in this book well illustrate Frauley's (2015a) point that criminology is about ordering more than it is about crime. We focus on imprisonment in Chapter 4, but other than that our topics are not about the criminal justice system. Other forms of confinement and containment, such as children's homes, Magdalene laundries and refugee camps illustrate how the net of coercive control was and is much wider than the criminal justice system. They also exemplify how people are not only confined for committing crimes, and how the purpose of confinement is not necessarily punishment. Rather, confinement and containment are practices of social ordering, securing boundaries of race, gender and sexuality, and nationality and citizenship. This is why we take transgression – the crossing of boundaries – as our organising concept (O'Neill and Seal, 2012). Significantly, we argue that transgression is not always conscious or deliberate. It can be an act of defiance but it may also result from falling on the wrong side of a boundary due to cultural norms, social position and lack of structural privilege or, as in Chapter 5, the shifting social and legal boundaries of refugee regimes and the governance of those on the move in 'negative globalisation'.

In addition to the use of creative methodologies, our other priority in this book has been to assess how the imagination and organisation of space is crucial to social ordering as it demarcates boundaries of inclusion and exclusion. Confinement in institutions removes certain groups from the population and/or heavily restricts their movement and presence in wider society. Containment in refugee camps prevents non-citizens' entry into the societies of the countries in which they arrive. Chapter 6 examines how the spatialisation of social order is also secured in urban landscapes via walls and boundaries. In Belfast, the 'architecture of conflict' means that there are physical barriers between different areas but also invisible lines between loyalist and republican areas that cannot be crossed. Not all of the physical barriers are fences and solid walls – they can also be car parks or shopping centres deliberately placed to demarcate one area from another. The residents of the DTES in Vancouver – historically its 'skid row' – were poor, marginalised and Indigenous, and the area separated them from the rest of the city. Gentrification is leading to the reorganisation of this space to exclude its longer-term residents. The alternative societies imagined in the novels discussed in Chapter 7 depict how authoritarian regimes and oligarchies use spatial organisation and segregation as a tool of governance and to secure power – our other examples underline how liberal democracies also govern via forms of spatial regulation.

Walking methodologies are particularly suitable for the appreciation and analysis of space but imagining space also takes place through practising creative arts, acts of remembering and consuming cultural forms such as films and novels. We have explored how space is imagined in multiple and contradictory ways; sites may be associated with trauma but also with fond childhood memories, for example. Even institutions can become 'eulogised space' (Bachelard, 1994) if they provided some happy times or had beautiful areas such as gardens that offered respite from institutional buildings. In discussing prison creative writing classes, we highlighted how prisons can have some areas which are less prison-like than others, such as the library, which facilitate different types of interactions and interrelations than the wings. Different, concurrent experiences of the same spaces are also significant as Chapter 6's analysis of urban space makes clear. Space generates multiple meanings and stories (Massey, 1999).

Our focus on social ordering via spatial organisation means that we have paid close attention to geographies of domination and resistance. State, and other forms of power, are enacted spatially but there is also resistance and protest. The Women's Memorial March in Vancouver is a prime example but so is the daily survival of individuals in extreme circumstances, such as refugee camps, who must employ tricks and tactics to navigate their containment. The imagination also provides a route to resistance – of imagining oneself beyond one's current situation and into a hopeful future, whether through creative outputs, such as writing poems and stories, or through accessing other worlds and experiences through reading and viewing.

Imaginative criminology and theoretical developments

Cultural and critical criminology have analysed how capitalism shapes and reproduces social ordering and cultural geographers have highlighted how the urban landscape is organised according to capitalist priorities. Our examples demonstrate how criminologists also need to pay greater attention to legacies of Western colonialism (which are intertwined with structures of capitalism, see Getachew, 2018) as these are so deeply embedded in social ordering, social regulation and the movement of people. Cunneen and Tauri (2016) identify colonialism as a continuing 'void' in criminology although this is beginning to change. Colonial legacies quite clearly shape contemporary criminal justice systems in terms of the racialisation of laws, policing and punishment. Widening the criminological lens to transgression and ordering of space entails encountering the significance of colonialism to other forms of confinement, to Western countries' treatment of refugees and newcomers and, as in Belfast, to the spatial organisation of the city. Our chapters that consider children's homes in Australia and Vancouver's DTES highlight both how colonial power has devastated Indigenous people's communities historically and how it continues to do so. Fundamentally, our contemporary world's borders, its global disparities of wealth, the movement of peoples and the election of governments directly result from colonial and postcolonial histories. Criminologists must continue to extend their work to recognise this.

This book also illuminates analysis of memory and forgetting, both on the personal and collective levels, as crucial to imaginative criminology. As with colonialism, memory and forgetting have strong conceptual potential for criminologists but are not explored in depth by much work in the discipline (historical criminology is obviously something of an exception although does not necessarily address memory per se). Social ordering, the regulation of transgression and the lived experience of transgression all have histories which also bear on the present, as our examples show in a multitude of ways. They live on in individual and cultural memory, in presence and absences within the landscape and at particular sites. Which stories and histories get to be told, and when it becomes possible to tell them, are vital questions for criminologists to consider. Chapter 7 examined how dystopian young adult fiction highlights both the suppression of memory as an authoritarian tactic and its recovery as having subversive potential. Attention to place in history can invigorate the criminological imagination, and creative methodologies, coupled with historical awareness, are a means to do this (drawing on Adorno and Benjamin, O'Neill (1999) calls the combination of social science research and art making 'ethno-mimesis', O'Neill and Seal, 2012). We return to Adorno's (2005: 89) dictum to 'not close the books on the past'. The example of colonialism is a pertinent one. Its violent past is largely forgotten in the public spheres of former colonial powers such as Britain, and this forgetting is evident in western criminology too (see King, 2017).

The public role of imaginative criminology

Imaginative criminology lends itself well to being public criminology. Participatory arts-based methods engage their participants and entail doing research 'with' rather than 'on', making them more democratic than conventional social science research methods. In this book and in *Transgressive Imaginations* (O'Neill and Seal, 2012), we have shown how creative approaches and the art work, writing, performances and walks they produce have greater potential to reach, include and engage wider audiences than does 'academic' writing alone. They also encourage multi-sensory ways of knowing, feeling and remembering.

As we have explored, cultural representations are constitutive of cultural memory and are incredibly important to understand in relation to the place of historical actors, events and processes in the public sphere. As portrayals that live in the public domain, they are important sources for criminologists to grapple with. Cultural representations, including fiction, are also powerful learning tools for developing critical pedagogies with students and wider publics (O'Neill, 2001; Frauley, 2010). They enable thinking through and beyond transgression, ordering and power as well as the imagination of different worlds and possibilities. Sociological facts, as Gordon (1997: 26) notes, are 'always in imminent danger of being contaminated by what is seemingly on the other side of their boundaries, by fictions'. Rather than disavowing the contamination of fiction, sociologists and criminologists must embrace its promise for enhancing creative thinking.

This imagining of different worlds and possibilities is vital for imaginative criminology. In her genre-crossing book *Carceral Capitalism*, Wang (2018: 298) exhorts us to use 'a mode of thinking that does not capitulate to the Present'. When we become mired in realism, it is difficult to think past existing social relations and institutions. We dismiss attempts to do so as naively utopian and unrealistic. She urges 'the re-enchantment of the world' as the way to set about unthinking the injustices of the present (2018: 298). This re-enchantment is vital for criminologists not only to envision the future, but also to pay attention to the 'magic of social reality', to the hidden, the half-submerged and the repressed (Gordon, 1997: 203).

Transformative justice and the radical democratic imaginary: towards undisciplining criminology?

We closed *Transgressive Imaginations* by offering an invitation to develop an agenda for cultural criminology towards a public criminology for the 21st century that involved engaging wider audiences and working with different publics through critical, cultural and participatory methods. This was underpinned by four key points that were inspired by Bauman (2011): de-familiarise the familiar; only connect, show the interconnections through interdisciplinarity and transdisiplinary working; unravel doxa – think critically and dialectically; but importantly use multi-sensory ways of thinking, listening, seeing and feeling. It is crucial to open and keep open dialogue that fosters mutual trust and subject-subject relationalities, uncovers hidden histories and values the knowledge in communities. This necessarily entails a kind of *undisciplining* of criminology[1] that also involves a focus on the colonial (see Mayblin, 2017). In this, our second book, we have developed this agenda by focusing specifically upon space and spatial analyses, which also involves time and the relational, and seeks to open and keep open spaces for a radical democratic imaginary alongside the radical democratic potential of imaginative criminology.

---

[1] We borrow here the use of 'Undisciplining' from *The Sociological Review*'s recent conference of that name, 18–21 June 2018, Gateshead.

Imaginative Criminology builds upon our earlier focus on representing crime through analyses of cultural constructions of transgression, to imagining crime and what an imaginative criminology might look and feel like, if we take seriously our interdisciplinary and transdisciplinary agenda. We have taken forward in this book our commitment to the imaginary domain 'as a moral and psychic space' that is necessary in order to open, keep open and rework the 'repressed elements of the imaginary' (Cornell, 2006: 31) through a focus upon space and a politics that opens itself up to the spatial and the relational. Drawing upon Gatens and Lloyd (1999) and Grossberg (1996), Massey (1999: 188) suggests that thinking spatially forces us to think about ourselves in relation to others in ways that temporal thinking does not. In Massey's (1999) analysis of space, as we have discussed earlier, there is a political importance to acknowledging that being open to the future involves understanding that 'time-space' and 'space [are] always being made' (1999: 189). This openness must also pay attention to relationships, relationalities, the spatiality of politics and the spatiality of our responsibility to others. This spatial approach to time-space and politics that is also relational connects with our work on the possibilities of and for a radical democratic imaginary and how this might facilitate or foster both imaginative criminology and transformative justice.

Imaginative criminology that involves creative methods and spatial analyses would necessarily situate the lived experiences, voices and biographies at the centre of knowledge production through micrology and advance better understandings of crime, social harm, justice and punishment, and their ordering and organisation. Hence the importance of creating and ensuring space for democratic contestation and anti-essentialism, founded on 'the circulation, radicalisation and institutionalisation of democratic discourse' (Smith, 1998: 7); the critical recovery of hidden histories; and our collaborative, participatory and arts-based methods. We have argued that multivocal, dialogical texts can make visible emotional structures and inner experiences which may 'move' audiences through what can be described as 'sensuous knowing' or mimesis. The 'subjective-reflexive' feeling involved in the process of creating/producing arts-based work can also be change causing for the producer and can be therapeutic/healing for the artist and audience. The process involved in the practice of 'ethno-mimesis' is reflexive and phenomenological but it is also critical and looks to praxis.

Our spatial and relational approach to imaginative criminology argues for a public criminology that makes possible a radical democratic imaginary, which in turn incorporates transformative justice. Here we value Hudson's (2006) principles of social justice. Her emphasis on the need for justice to recognise plurality, diversity and difference is vitally important for an imaginative criminology of space that extends our earlier work on transgressive imaginations. The three principles we incorporate into our analysis here (underpinned by our feminist, critical race theory and de-colonising approach) are that justice should include discursiveness, relationalism and reflectiveness (Hudson, 2006: 35–9). To these we add a fourth principle – understandings of space and the spatial. How then do these principles relate to imaginative criminology as presented in this book?

First, the discursive aspect of justice means that those most excluded from justice should be given privileged access to discourse because the 'outsider' must be able to put their claims in their own terms and not have to accommodate to the dominant modes of legal/political discourse (Hudson, 2006). Importantly people must be given the space to tell their story in their own words. Second, the relational aspect of justice recognises that we are social and relational beings and our identities are situationally and relationally contingent. Justice needs to incorporate an awareness and understanding of the relational, our embeddedness in networks and relationships that give meaning to our lives. Rights are also relational for Hudson (2006: 37). Third, the reflective aspect of justice means 'that each case should be considered in terms of all its subjectivities, harms, wrongs and contexts, and then measured against concepts such as oppression, freedom, dignity and equality' (Hudson, 2006: 39). For Hudson a more reflective version of justice means considering the particulars of a unique case against these broader issues because without such reflection justice collapses into one-dimensionality and then closure. For example, she argues that the abstract generality of law, where acts have to be fitted into certain categories, means that liberal justice expels difference around individual biographies, situational circumstances and subjectivity. Moreover, relational and reflective principles are closely related to discursiveness and must be incorporated 'if discursiveness is to move beyond the closures of established justice, beyond the fixed identities and categories of dominant legal discourse' (Hudson, 2006: 39).

Challenging oppression, inequality and domination could guide the practical implementation of justice policies and processes, through championing discursiveness, relationalism and reflection in our research and practice.[2] In advancing this argument, we want to include

---

[2] O'Neill and Laing (2018) operationalise Hudson's arguments here in relation to sex work.

spatial dimensions of justice. Fourth, the spatial dimension of justice involves the spatial, situational contexts in which meanings are made and the ways that space is constantly being made (Massey, 1999). This means we need to attend to the fact that multiple meanings and stories are generated across the discursive, relational, reflective and spatial elements of justice. In doing justice we take into account, as we have in this book, the various spaces of control or confinement (Magdalene laundries, prisons, refugee camps and care homes); the borders both real and imagined that produce liminal betwixt-and-between spaces and places (peace walls and border lines), as well as fictional dystopias. We have discussed how these spaces are experienced, understood, imagined and remembered.

Taken together, the principles of discursiveness, reflection, the relational and the spatial can not only combine to provide a more holistic concept of social justice, but can also facilitate and promote a radical democratic imaginary. Building upon our earlier work on transgression, a radical democratic imaginary as part of imaginative criminology opens and keeps open a space for repressed elements of the imaginary, for transgressive imaginations, and develops more spatial (alongside relational, reflective and discursive) understandings of social justice, as transformative justice. We return to our opening point that an imaginative approach is necessary in order to comprehend the complexity of issues of transgression and space, to understand, facilitate and do justice and to ensure the continued reinvigoration of criminology as a discipline.

References

Abdi, AM (2006) 'Refugee, Gender Based Violence and Resistance' in E Tassioglou and A Dobrowlesky (eds) *Women, Migration and Citizenship*, London: Routledge.

Adams, A (1999) Alice Adams interviewed by Colleen Brown for the Bringing them home oral history project [sound recording] Oral TRC 1349597: http://nla.gov.au/nla.obj-218183501/listen

Adelman, H (1999) 'Modernity, Globalization, Refugees and Displacement', in A Ager (ed) *Refugees: Perspectives on the experience of enforced migration*, London: Continuum, pp 83–110.

Adorno, A (1978) *Mimima Moralia: Reflections on a Damaged Life*, London: Verso.

Adorno, T (2005) 'The Meaning of Working Through the Past' in *Critical Models: Interventions and Catchwords*, New York, Columbia University Press.

Agamben, G (1995) *Homo Sacer: Sovereign Power and Bare Life*, Stanford, CA, Stanford University Press.

Amin, A (2006) Collective Culture and Urban Public Space: http://publicspace.org/en/text-library/eng/b003-collective-culture-and-urban-public-space.

Amin, A (2013) 'Telescopic Urbanism and the Poor', *City*, 17(4): 476–92.

Anderson, B (1983) *Imagined Communities: Reflections on the Origin and Spread of Nationalism*, London: Verso.

Arendt, H (1970) *On Violence*, New York: Harcourt Brace.

Arendt, H (1994) *Essays in Understanding*, London: Harcourt, Brace & Company.

Atwood, M (2003) *Oryx and Crake*, London: Bloomsbury.

Bachelard, G (1994) *The Poetics of Space*, Boston, MA: Beacon Press. 2nd edition.

Bachman, R [King, S] (1982) *The Running Man*, New York: Signet Books.

Back, L and Puwar, N (eds) (2012) *Live Methods*, London: The Sociological Review Monograph, Wiley.

Badagliacco, JM and Ruiz, CD (2006) 'Impoverished Appalachia and Kentucky Genomes: What Is at Stake? How Do Feminists Reply?', *New Genetics and Society*, 25(2): 209–26.

Bagndi, A (2009) 'Beyond the Standard Interview: the Use of Graphic Elicitation and Arts-based Methods', *Qualitative Research*, 9(5): 547–70.

Bailly, AS (1993) 'Spatial Imaginary and Geography', *GeoJournal*, 31(3): 24–50.

Bancroft, KH (2012) 'Zones of Exclusion: Urban Spatial Policies, Social Justice and Social Services', *Journal of Sociology and Social Welfare*, 39(3): 63–84.

Barthes, R (1981) *Camera Lucida: Reflections on Photography*, New York: Hill and Wang.

Barton, A, Corteen, K, Scott, D and Whyte, D (2007) *Expanding the Criminological Imagination: Critical Readings in Criminology*, Cullompton: Willan.

Basu, B (2013) 'What Faction Are You In? The Pleasure of Being Sorted in Veronica Roth's *Divergent*', in B Basu, KR Broad and C Hintz (eds) *Brave New Teenagers*, New York: Routledge, pp 19–33.

Basu, B, Broad, KR and Hintz, C (2013) 'Introduction' in B Basu, KR Broad and C Hintz (eds) *Brave New Teenagers*, New York: Routledge, pp 1–15.

Baudrillard, J (1991) 'Simulacra and Science Fiction', *Science Fiction Studies*, 18(3): 309–13.

Baudrillard, J (1993) 'Hyperreal America', *Economy and Society*, 22(2): 243–52.

Bauman, Z (2001) *Community*, Cambridge: Polity Press.

Bauman, Z (2004) *Wasted Lives: Modernity and Its Outcasts*, Cambridge: Polity Press.

Bauman, Z (2007) *Liquid Times: Living in an Age of Uncertainty*, Cambridge: Polity Press.

Bauman, Z (2011) 'Reflections on Economy and Society', public lecture at Durham University, 16 February. Chaired by Prof. Roy Boyne.

Beaumont, C (1997) 'Women, Citizenship and Catholicism in the Irish Free State, 1922–1948', *Women's History Review*, 6(4): 563–85.

Becker, HS (1963) *Outsiders: Studies in the Sociology of Deviance*, Glencoe: The Free Press.

Belfast Interface Project (2011) https://www.belfastinterfaceproject.org/interfaces-map-and-database-overview

Benhabib, S (2004). *The Rights of Others: Aliens, Residents, and Citizens*, Cambridge: Cambridge University Press.

Bennett, A (1981) 'Cold Sweat', *London Review of Books*, 3(19): 12–13.

Beyer, C (2010) 'Exploring Postcolonial and Feminist Issues: *Rabbit Proof Fence* in a Teaching Context', *Changing English*, 17(1): 93–101.

Bilby, C, Caulfield, L and Ridley, L (2013) *Reimagining Futures: Exploring Arts Interventions and the Process of Desistance*, London: Arts Alliance.

Bissell, D (2016) 'Micropolitics of Mobility: Public Transport Commuting and Everyday Encounters with Forces of Enablement And constraint', *Annals of the American Association of Geographers*, 106(2): 394–403.

Black, L (2018) '"On the other hand the accused is a woman…": Women and the Death Penalty in Post-independence Ireland', *Law and History Review*, 36(1): 139–72.

Bloomfield, G (2001) George Bloomfield interviewed by John Maynard for the Bringing them home oral history project [sound recording] Oral TRC 887596: http://nla.gov.au/nla.obj-218398674/listen

Blue (2014) Dir Gabi, A [Film]: https://www.youtube.com/watch?v=gi4PzuOI10w.

Bosworth M (2008) 'Border Control and the Limits of the Sovereign State', *Social & Legal Studies*, 17(2): 199–215.

Branch, D (2005) 'Imprisonment and Colonialism in Kenya, c. 1930–1952: Escaping the Carceral Archipelago', *International Journal of African Historical Studies*, 38(2): 239–65.

Breakell, S (2008) 'Perspectives: Negotiating the Archive', *Tate Papers*, 9: ISSN 1753-9854.

Bringing Them Home: Report of the National Inquiry into the Separation of Aboriginal and Torres Strait Islander Children from their Families (1997) Sydney: Human Rights and Equal Opportunity Commission.

Broad, KR (2013) '"The Dandelion in the Spring": Utopia as Romance in Suzanne Collins's The Hunger Games Trilogy', in B Basu, KR Broad and C Hintz (eds) *Brave New Teenagers*, New York: Routledge, pp 117–30.

Brown, A (2003) *English Society and the Prison: Time, Culture and Politics in the Development of the Modern Prison, 1850–1920*, Woodbridge: The Boydell Press.

Brown, M (2009) *The Culture of Punishment: Prison, Society and Spectacle*, New York: New York University Press.

Brown, P (2014) *Red Rising*, New York: Del Rey Books.

Bull, KB (2012) 'Identifying Obstacles and Garnering Support: Young Adult Literature in the English Arts Classroom', in JA Hayn and JS Kaplan (eds) *Teaching Young Adult Literature Today: Insights, Considerations and Perspectives for the Classroom Teacher*, Lanham, MD: Rowman and Littlefield, pp 61–78.

Burgess, A (1962) *A Clockwork Orange*, London: William Heinemann.

Burgess, E (1928) 'Residential Segregation in American Cities', *The Annals of the American Academy of Political Science and Social Science*, 140: 105–15.

Byrne, DR (2003) 'Nervous Landscapes: Race and Space in Australia', *Journal of Social Archaeology*, 3(2): 169–93.

Cain, D (2004) 'A Fence Too Far?' *Third Text*, 18(4): 297–303.

Campbell, E (2013) 'Transgression, Affect and Performance: Choreographing a Politics of Urban Space', *British Journal of Criminology*, 53(1): 18–40.

Campbell, E (2016) 'Policing Paedophilia: Assembling Bodies, Spaces and Things', *Crime, Media, Culture*, 12(3): 345–65.

Capuano, PJ (2003) 'Truth in Timbre: Morrison's Extension of Slave Narrative Song in "Beloved"', *African American Review*, 37(1): 95–103.

Carlen, P (2008) 'Imaginary Penalities and Risk-crazed Governance', in P Carlen (ed) *Imaginary Penalities*, Cullompton: Willan, pp 1–25.

Carlen, P (2010) *A Criminological Imagination*, London: Ashgate.

Carlen, P (2017) 'Doing Imaginative Criminology', in *Liquid Criminology: Doing Imaginative Criminological Research*, London: Routledge, pp 17–30.

Carlen, P, Hicks, J, O'Dwyer, J, Christina, D, Tchaikovsky, C (1985). *Criminal Women: Autobiographical Accounts*, Cambridge: Polity Press.

Carrabine, E (2012) 'Just Images: Aesthetics, Ethics and Visual Criminology', *British Journal of Criminology*, 52(3): 463–89.

Carrabine, E (2018) 'Punishment in the Frame: Rethinking the History and Sociology of Art', *The Sociological Review*, 66(3): 559–76.

Castles, S (2003) 'Towards a Sociology of Forced Migration and Social Transformation', *Sociology* 37(1): 13–34.

Castoriadis, C (1987) *The Imaginary Institution of Society*, Oxford: Blackwell.

Chandra-Shekeran, S (1998) 'Challenging the Fiction of the Nation in the "Reconciliation" Texts of Mabo and Bringing Them Home', *Australian Feminist Law Journal*, 11(1): 107–33.

Cheliotis, L and Jordanoska, A (2016) 'The Arts of Desistance: Assessing the Role of Arts-based Programmes in Reducing Reoffending', *The Howard Journal*, 55(1/2): 25–41.

Choo, C (2002) 'Sister Kate's Home for "Nearly White" Children', in A Haebich and D Mellor (eds) *Many Voices: Reflections on Experiences of Indigenous Child Separation*, Canberra: National Library of Australia, pp 193–212.

Clark, B (2006) *Twice a Stranger: How Mass Expulsion Forged Modern Greece and Turkey*, London: Granta Books.

Clark, I (2002) 'Indigenous Children and Institutions', in A Haebich and D Mellor (eds) *Many Voices: Reflections on Experiences of Indigenous Child Separation*, Canberra: National Library of Australia, pp 165–76.

Clarke, J (2001) 'The Pleasures of Crime: Interrogating the Detective Story', in J Muncie and E McLaughlin (eds) *The Problem of Crime*, London: Sage, pp 72–106.

Clemente, A, Higgins, MJ and Sughrua, WM (2011) 'I Don't Find Any Privacy Around Here: Ethnographic Encounters with Legal Practices of Literacy in the State Prison of Oaxaca', *Language and Education*, 25(6): 491–513.

Clements, P (2004) 'The Rehabilitative Role of Arts Education in Prison: Accommodation or Enlightenment?', *International Journal of Art and Design Education*, 23(2): 169–78.

Cohen, S (1971) *Images of Deviance*, London: Penguin.

Collins, S (2008) *The Hunger Games*, New York: Scholastic.

Collyer, M (2010) 'Stranded Migrants and the Fragmented Journey', *Journal of Refugee Studies*, 23(3): 273–93.

Conlon, D, Heimstra, N and Mountz, A (2017) Spatial Control: Geographical Approaches to the Study of Immigration. The Global Detention Project Working Paper Series. Geneva, Switzerland.

Cornell, D (1995) *The Imaginary Domain*, London: Routledge

Cornell, D (1998) *At the Heart of Freedom: Feminism, Sex and Equality*, Princeton, NJ: Princeton University Press.

Cornell, D (2006) 'An interview with Drucilla Cornell' in R Heberle (ed) *Feminist Interpretations of Theodor Adorno*, Penn State University Press.

Couzelis, MJ (2013) 'The Future Is Pale: Race in Contemporary Young Adult Dystopian Novels', in B Basu, KR Broad and C Hintz (eds) *Brave New Teenagers*, New York: Routledge, pp 131–44.

Cox, A and Gelsthorpe, L (2012) 'Creative Encounters: Whatever Happened to the Arts in Prisons', in L Cheliotis (ed) *The Arts of Imprisonment: An Introduction*, Farnham: Ashgate.

Cresswell, T (1996) *In Place/Out of Place: Geography, Ideology and Transgression*, Minneapolis, MN: University of Minnesota Press.

Crewe, B, Warr, J, Bennett, P and Smith, A (2014) 'The Emotional Geography of Prison Life', *Theoretical Criminology*, 18(1): 56–74.

Crowley, U and Kitchin, R (2008) 'Producing "Decent Girls": Governmentality and the Moral Geographies of Sexual Conduct in Ireland (1922–1937)', *Gender, Place and Culture*, 15(4): 355–72.

Cunneen, C (1999) 'Criminology, Genocide and the Forced Removal of Indigenous Children from Their Families', *Australian and New Zealand Journal of Criminology*, 32(2): 124–38.

Cunneen, C (2016) 'When Does Transitional Justice Begin and End? Colonised Peoples, Liberal Democracies and Restorative Justice', in K Clamp (ed) *Restorative Justice in Transitional Settings*, Abingdon: Routledge, pp 190–210.

Cunneen, C and Tauri, J (2016) *Indigenous Criminology*, Bristol: Policy Press.

Cursley, J and Maruna, S (2015) A Narrative Based Evaluation of 'Changing Tunes' Music Based Prisoner Reintegration Interventions: http://www.artsevidence.org.uk/media/uploads/final-report-cursley-and-maruna-changing-tunes.pdf.

Cuthbert, D and Quartly, M (2013) 'Forced Child Removal and the Politics of National Apologies in Australia', *American Indian Quarterly*, 37(1/2): 178–202.

Dashner, J (2009) *The Maze Runner*, New York: Delacorte Press.

Datta, A (2013) 'Encounters with Law and Critical Urban Studies. Reflections on Amin's Telescopic Urbanism', *City*, 17(4): 517–22.

Davey, K (2015) Using Archives Within the Criminal Justice System: A Case Study, London: National Alliance for the Arts in Criminal Justice: https://www.artsincriminaljustice.org.uk/wp-content/uploads/2016/07/case-study-3-university-of-sussex.pdf.

Day, H (2012) 'Simulacra, Sacrifice and Survival in The Hunger Games, Battle Royale and The Running Man', in MF Pharr and LA Clark (eds) *Of Bread, Blood and the Hunger Games*, Jefferson, NC: McFarland, pp 167–78.

de Certeau, M (1985) 'Practices of Space', in M Blonsky (ed) *Signs*, Baltimore, MD: Johns Hopkins University Press, pp 122–46.

Diener, AC and Hagan, J (2012) *Borders: A Very Short Introduction*, Oxford: Oxford University Press.

Dodgshon, RA (2008) 'Geography's Place in Time', *Geografiska Annaler: Series B*, 90(1): 1–15.

Domosh, M (1998) 'Those "Gorgeous Incongruities": Polite Politics and Public Spaces on the Streets of Nineteenth Century New York City', *Annals of the Association of American Geographers*, 88(2): 209–26.

Donnelly, R (1998) 'Helpline callers express anger and distress', *The Irish Times*, 20 March, p 2.

Edensor, T (2010) 'Walking in Rhythms: place, regulation, style and the flow of experience', *Visual Studies*, 25(1): 46–58.

Elliot, A (2015) 'Power in Our Words: Finding Community and Mitigating Trauma in James Dashner's The Maze Runner', *Children's Literature Association Quarterly*, 40(2): 179–99.

Erikson, KT (1962) 'Notes on the Sociology of Deviance', *Social Problems*, 9: 307–14.

Fals Borda, O (1999) (1988) *Knowledge and People's Power: Lessons with Peasants in Nicaragua, Mexico and Columbia*, New York: New Horizons Press.

Fischer, C (2016) 'Gender, Nation, and the Politics of Shame: Magdalen Laundries and the Institutionalization of Feminine Transgression in Modern Ireland', *Signs*, 41(4): 821–43.

Fiske, J (2010) *Understanding Popular Culture*, London: Routledge. 2nd edition.

Fleetwood, J. (2014). *Drug Mules: Women in the International Cocaine Trade*, Basingstoke: Macmillan.

Foucault, M (1979) *Discipline and Punish: The Birth of the Prison*, London: Penguin.

Foucault, M (1986) 'Of Other Spaces', *Diacritics*, 16(1): 22–27.

Franklin, HB (2008) 'The Inside Stories of the Global American Prison', *Texas Studies in Literature and Language*, 50(3): 235–42.

Frauley, J (2010) *Criminology, Deviance and the Silver Screen: The Fictional Reality and the Criminological Imagination*, New York: Palgrave.

Frauley, J (2015a) 'On Imaginative Criminology and Its Significance', *Societies*, 5(3): 618–30.

Frauley, J (2015b) 'C Wright Mills and the Criminological Imagination: Introductory Remarks', in J Frauley (ed) *C Wright Mills and the Criminological Imagination: Prospects for Creative Inquiry*, Farnham: Ashgate, pp 13–24.

Fulton, H (2010) 'Walk', in S Pink, P Hubbard, M O'Neill and A Radley (eds) Walking Ethnography and Arts Practice (Special Issue), *Visual Studies*, 25(1): 8–14

Gabi, A (2014) *Blue* [Film] https://www.youtube.com/watch?v=gi4PzuOI10w.

Garde-Hansen, J (2011) *Media and Memory*, Edinburgh: Edinburgh University Press.

Gatens, M and Lloyd, G (1999) *Collective Imaginings: Spinoza Past and Present*, London: Routledge.

Getachew, A (2018) '"The Welfare World", Evil Empire: A Reckoning with Power', *Boston Review*, Fall: 30–40.

Goffman, E [1961] (2007) *Asylums: Essays on the Social Situation of Mental Patients and Other Inmates*, New Brunswick: Aldine Transaction.

Golding, W (1954) *Lord of the Flies*, London: Faber and Faber.

Gordon, A (1997) *Ghostly Matters: Haunting and Sociological Imagination*, Minneapolis, MN: University of Minnesota Press.

Graham, S (2000) Syd Graham interviewed by Karen George in the Bringing them home oral history project [sound recording], Oral TRC 942394: http://nla.gov.au/nla.obj-218413589/listen.

Green-Barteet, MA (2014) '"I'm beginning to know who I am": The Rebellious Subjectivities of Katniss Everdeen and Tris Prior', in SK Day, MA Green-Barteet and AL Montz (eds) *Female Rebellion in Young Adult Fiction*, London: Routledge, pp 33–49.

Grierson, J (2017) 'Mass Grave of Babies and Children Found at Tuam Care Home Ireland', *The Guardian*, 3 March: https://www.theguardian.com/world/2017/mar/03/mass-grave-of-babies-and-children-found-at-tuam-orphanage-in-ireland.

Grossberg, L (1996) 'The Space of Culture, The Power of Place' in I Chambers and L Curti (eds) *The Postcolonial Question*, London: Routledge.

Gyollai, D and Amatrudo, A (2018) 'Controlling Irregular Migration: International Human Rights Standards and the Hungarian Legal Framework', *European Journal of Criminology*, https://doi.org/10.1177/1477370818772776: 1–20.

Hardt, M (1997) 'Prison Time', *Yale French Studies*, 91: 64–79.

Harrison, H (2000) Harold Harrison interviewed by Rob Willis for the Bringing them home oral history project [sound recording] Oral TRC 330519: http://nla.gov.au/nla.obj-218245894/listen.

Hart, M (2001) Marie Hart interviewed by Lily Bhavna Kauler for the Bringing them home oral history project [sound recording] Oral TRC 5947: http://nla.gov.au/nla.obj-218492264/listen.

Hayward, K (2004) 'Space – The Final Frontier: Criminology, the City and the Spatial Dynamics of Exclusion', in J Ferrell, K Hayward, W Morrison and M Presdee (eds) *Cultural Criminology Unleashed*, London: Glasshouse Press, pp 155–66.

Hayward, K (2010) 'Opening the Lens: Cultural Criminology and the Image', in K Hayward and M Presdee (eds) *Framing Crime: Cultural Criminology and the Image*, Abingdon: Routledge, pp 1–16.

Hayward, KJ (2012) 'Five Spaces of Cultural Criminology', *British Journal of Criminology*, 52(3): 441–62.

Heddon, DE (2008) *Autobiography and Performance*, Palgrave Macmillan.

Hind, C and Qualmann, C (2015) *Ways to Wander*, Axminster: Triarchy Press.

Hinton, J (2010) *Nine Wartime Lives: Mass-Observation and the Making of the Modern Self*, Oxford: Oxford University Press.

Hinton-Smith, T and Seal, L (2018) 'Peformativity, Border-Crossings and Ethics in a Prison-Based Creative Writing Project', *Qualitative Research*, https://doi.org/10.1177/1468794118778975.

Hintz, C and Ostry E (2003) 'Introduction', in C Hintz and E Ostry (eds) *Utopian and Dystopian Writing for Children and Young Adults*, London: Routledge, pp 1–22.

Hogg, R (2001) 'Penality and Modes of Regulating Indigenous Peoples in Australia', *Punishment & Society*, 3(3): 355–79.

Honigmann, D (1991) 'A Perfectly Amiable Cherub from the Asylum', *The Independent*, 7 April, p 30.

Hubbard, P, Kitchin, R, Bartley, B and Fuller, D (2002) *Thinking Geographically*, London: Continuum.

Hudson, B (2006) 'Beyond White Man's Justice: Race Gender and Justice in Late Modernity', *Theoretical Criminology*, 10(1): 29–47.

Ingold, T and Vergunst, J (eds.) (2008) *Ways of Walking: Ethnography and Practice on Foot*, Aldershot: Ashgate.

Jacobs, J (2005) *Dark Age Ahead*, Toronto: Random House.

Jacobsen, MH (2014) 'Introduction: Towards the Poetics of Crime: Contours of a Cultural, Critical and Creative Criminology', in MH Jacobsen (ed) *The Poetics of Crime: Understanding and Researching Deviance*, Farnham: Ashgate, pp 1–25.

Jefferson, AM (2014) 'Conceptualizing Confinement: Prisons and Poverty in Sierra Leone', *Criminology and Criminal Justice*, 14(1): 44–60.

Jenks, C (2003) *Transgression*, London: Routledge.

Jewkes, Y (2013) 'On Carceral Space and Agency', in D Moran, N Gill and D Conlon (eds) *Carceral Spaces: Mobility and Agency in Prison and Migrant Detention*, London: Routledge, pp 127–31.

Johnson, LM (2008) 'A Place for Art in Prison: Art as a Tool for Rehabilitation and Management', *Southwest Journal of Criminal Justice*, 5(2): 100–20.

Johnson, P (2013) 'The Geographies of Heterotopia', *Geography Compass*, 7(11): 790–803.

Johnson, R (2012) 'Art and Autonomy: Prison Writers Under Siege', in L Cheliotis (ed) *The Arts of Imprisonment: An Introduction*, Farnham: Ashgate, pp 167–88.

Johnson, R and Chernoff, N (2002) '"Opening a Vein": Inmate Poetry and the Prison Experience', *The Prison Journal*, 82(2): 141–67.

Kandiyoti, D (1988) 'Bargaining with Patriarchy', *Gender and Society*, 2(3): 274–90.

Kapoor, N (2018) *Deport, Deprive, Extradite*, London: Verso.

Kennedy, R (2004) 'The Affective Work of Stolen Generations Testimony: From the Archives to the Classroom', *Biography*, 27(1): 48–77.

Kennedy, R (2008) 'Vulnerable Children, Disposable Mothers: Holocaust and Stolen Generations Memoirs of Childhood', *Life Writing*, 5(2): 161–84.

Kindynis, T (2014) 'Ripping up the Map: Criminology and Cartography Reconsidered', *British Journal of Criminology*, 54(2): 222–43.

King, S (2017) 'Colonial Criminology: A Survey of What it Means and Why It's Important', *Sociology Compass*, 11(3): e12447.

No More Beyond (Dir Kispert, M, 2015) https://vimeo.com/131399936.

Klein, D (2016) 'Narrating a Different (Hi)story', *Interventions*, 18(4): 588–604.

Kofman, E, Phizacklea, A, Raghuram, P and Sales, R (2000) *Gender and International Migration in Europe: Employment, Politics and Welfare*, London: Routledge.

Kristeva, J (1982) *Powers of Horror: An Essay on Abjection*, trans. Leon S Roudiez, New York: Columbia UP.

Kushner, T and Knox, K (1999) *Refugees in an Age of Genocide*, London: Frank Cass.

Laclau, E and Mouffe, C (1985) *Hegemony and Socialist Strategy: Towards a Radical Democratic Politics*, London: Verso.

Leavy, P (2009) *Methods Meets Art: Arts-Based Research Practice*, New York: Guilford Press.

Lefebvre, H (1991) *The Production of Space*, Oxford: Blackwell.

Levy, A. (2015) 'Experiments in enforcement along Europe's eastern edge: Evidence of emerging economies of exclusion in Moldova', Paper presented at the AAG Annual Meeting: Chicago, Illinois, 24 April.

Liberty (2018) *A Guide to The Hostile Environment*. London: Liberty.

Lindner, E (2006) *Making Enemies: Humiliation and International Conflict*, Westport, CT and London: Praeger Security.

Linow, V (2000) Valerie Linow interviewed by Diana Rich for the Bringing them home oral history project [sound recording], Oral TRC 544098: http://nla.gov.au/nla.obj-218324339/listen.

Lonely Planet (2018) Belfast: https://www.lonelyplanet.com/ireland/northern-ireland/belfast/safety.

Long, R (1967) A Line Made by Walking: http://www.tate.org.uk/art/artworks/long-a-line-made-by-walking-ar00142 (accessed 23 September 2018).

Lorenzer, A. (2002) *What is Unconscious Phantasy?* Trans by Tobias Vollstedt, http://www.otherscene.org/pdf/Lorenzer-UnconsicousPhantasy.pdf accessed 15 February 2019.

Lovrod, M (2015) 'Narrow Escapes: Gendered Adolescent Resistance to Intergenerational Neo/colonial Violence Across Time and Space', *Rocky Mountain Review of Language and Literature*, 69(1): 68–86.

Lowman, J (1987) 'Taking Young Prostitutes Seriously', *Canadian Review of Sociology and Anthropology*, 24(1): 99–116.

Lowman, J (2000) 'Violence and the Outlaw Status of (Street) Prostitution in Canada', *Violence Against Women* 6(9): 987–1011.

Lowman, J (2011) 'Deadly Inertia: A History of Constitutional Challenges to Canada's *Criminal Code* Sections on Prostitution', *Beijing Law Review*, 2(2): 33–54.

'Magdalene Oral History Project' (no date), Justice for Magdalenes Research: http://jfmresearch.com/home/oralhistoryproject/ (accessed 11 February 2019).

Mansell, A (2001) Allan Mansell interviewed by Lyn McLeavy for the Bringing them home oral history project [sound recording] Oral TRC 1119000: http://nla.gov.au/nla.obj-218461107/listen.

Marfleet, P (2006) *Refugees in A Global Era*, Basingstoke: Palgrave Macmillan.

Martin, LL and Mitchelson, ML (2009) 'Geographies of Detention and Imprisonment: Interrogating Spatial Practices of Confinement, Discipline, Law, and State Power', *Geography Compass*, 3(1): 459–77.

Mass Observation Archive/Directive (MOA/Dir) 2618.5.881, Summer 1988.

Massey, D (1994) *Space, Place and Gender*, Cambridge: Polity Press.

Massey, D (1999) 'Philosophy and Politics of Spatiality: Some Considerations', *Geographische Zeitschrift*, 87(1): 1–12.

Massey, D (2005) *For Space*, London: Sage.

Mayblin, L (2017) *Asylum after Empire. Colonial Legacies in the Politics of Asylum Seeking*, London: Rowman and Littlefield.

Mbembe, A (2000) 'At the Edge of the World: Boundaries, Territoriality, and Sovereignty in Africa', *Public Culture*, 12(1): 259–84.

Mbembe, A (2003) 'Necropolitics', *Public Culture*, 15(1): 11–40 (trans. Libby Meintjes).

McCorkel, JA (1998) 'Going to the Crackhouse: Critical Space as a Form of Resistance in Total Institutions and Everyday Life', *Symbolic Interaction*, 21(3): 227–52.

McCormick, L (2005) 'Sinister Sisters? The Portrayal of Ireland's Magdalene Asylums in Popular Culture', *Cultural and Social History*, 2(3): 373–79.

McGarry, R and Keating M (2010) 'Auto/biography, personal testimony and epiphany moments: a case study in research-informed teaching', *Enhancing Learning in the Social Sciences*, 3(1): 1–31.

McGrath, P (1990) *Spider*, London: Poseidon Press.

McNeill, F, Anderson, K, Colvin, S, Overy, K, Sparks, R and Tett, L (2011) 'Inspiring Desistance? Arts Projects and "What Works"', *Justitiele Verkennigen*, 37(5) 80–101.

Medlicott, D (1999) 'Surviving in the Time Machine: Suicidal Prisoners and the Pains of Imprisonment', *Time and Society*, 8(2/3): 211–30.

Mellor, D and Haebich, A (2002) 'A Community of Voices', in A Haebich and D Mellor (eds) *Many Voices: Reflections on Experiences of Indigenous Child Separation*, Canberra: National Library of Australia, pp 3–16.

Michael, K (1999) Keiran Michael interviewed by Phillip Connors for the Bringing them home oral history project [sound recording] Oral TRC 229876: http://nla.gov.au/nla.obj-218207386/listen.

Mitchell, D (2000) *Cultural Geography: A Critical Introduction*, Oxford: Blackwell.

Molloy, D (2015) *Cultural Memory and Literature: Re-Imagining Australia's Past*, Leiden: Brill.

Moran, D (2012) '"Doing Time" in Carceral Space: Timespace and Carceral Geography', *Geografiska Annaler: Series B*, 94(4): 305–16.

Moran, D (2013) 'Between Outside and Inside? Prison Visiting Rooms as Liminal Carceral Spaces', *GeoJournal*, 78(2): 339–51.

Moran, D (2015) *Carceral Geography: Spaces and Practices of Incarceration*, Farnham: Ashgate.

Morrissey, TJ (2013) 'Parables for the Postmodern, Post 9/11, and Posthuman World', in B Basu, KR Broad and C Hintz (eds) *Brave New Teenagers*, New York: Routledge, pp 189–201.

Morton, L and Lounsbury, L (2015) 'Inertia to Action: From Narrative Empathy to Political Agency in Young Adult Fiction', *Papers: Explorations into Children's Literature*, 23(2): 53–70.

Mulhern, S (2015) *Ghosts of our Future*, Durham (Project Publication).

Muller, V (2012) 'Virtually Real: Suzanne Collins's *The Hunger Games* Trilogy', *International Research in Children's Literature*, 5(1): 51–63.

Myers, M (2010) 'Walk With Me, Talk with Me': The Art of Conversive Wayfinding, *Visual Studies,* 26(1): 50–68.

Nancy, J-L (2001) *Being Singular Plural*, Stanford CA: Stanford University Press.

Neary, S (2001) Sylvia Neary interviewed by Jane Watson for the Bringing them home oral history project [sound recording] Oral TRC 893601: http://nla.gov.au/nla.obj-218402746/listen.

O'Donnell, K, Pembroke, S and McGettrick, C (2013a) 'Oral History of Mary'. Magdalene Institutions: Recording an Oral and Archival History. Government of Ireland Collaborative Research Project, Irish Research Council, pp 1–60.

O'Donnell, K, Pembroke, S and McGettrick, C (2013b) 'Oral History of Lucy'. Magdalene Institutions: Recording an Oral and Archival History. Government of Ireland Collaborative Research Project, Irish Research Council, pp 1–88.

O'Donnell, K, Pembroke, S and McGettrick, C (2013c) 'Oral History of Evelyn'. Magdalene Institutions: Recording an Oral and Archival History. Government of Ireland Collaborative Research Project, Irish Research Council, pp 1–75.

O'Donnell, K, Pembroke, S and McGettrick, C (2013d) 'Oral History of Bernadette'. Magdalene Institutions: Recording an Oral and Archival History. Government of Ireland Collaborative Research Project, Irish Research Council, pp 1–107.

O'Donnell, K, Pembroke, S and McGettrick, C (2013e) 'Oral History of Mary Currington'. Magdalene Institutions: Recording an Oral and Archival History. Government of Ireland Collaborative Research Project, Irish Research Council, pp 1–116.

O'Donnell, K, Pembroke, S and McGettrick, C (2013f) 'Oral History of Chrissie Plunkett'. Magdalene Institutions: Recording an Oral and Archival History. Government of Ireland Collaborative Research Project, Irish Research Council, pp 1–70.

O'Donnell, K, Pembroke, S and McGettrick, C (2013g) 'Oral History of Pippa Flanagan'. Magdalene Institutions: Recording an Oral and Archival History. Government of Ireland Collaborative Research Project, Irish Research Council, pp 1–48.

O'Neill, M (1998) 'Saloon Girls: Death and Desire in the American West', in J Hassard and R Holliday (eds) *Organization-Representation: Work and Organization in Popular Culture*, London: Sage, pp 117–30.

O'Neill, M (1999) (ed) *Adorno, Culture and Feminism*, London: Sage.

O'Neill, M (2001) *Prostitution and Feminism: Towards a Politics of Feeling*, Cambridge: Polity Press.

O'Neill, M (2004) 'Crime, Culture and Visual Methodologies: Ethno-mimesis as Performative Praxis', In J Ferrell, K Hayward, W Morrisson and M Presdee (eds) *Cultural criminology unleashed*, London: Glasshouse Press.

O'Neill, M (2010) *Asylum, Migration and Community*, Bristol: Policy Press.

O'Neill, M (2011) 'Participatory Methods and Critical Models: Arts, Migration and Diaspora', *Crossings: Journal of Migration and Culture*, 2(1): 13–37.

O'Neill, M (2012) 'Ethno-Mimesis and Participatory Arts', in S Pink (ed) *Advances in Visual Methodology*, London: Sage.

O'Neill, M (2017) 'Studying the Marginalised using Mixed Methods', in MJ Jacobsen and S Walklate (ed) *Liquid Criminology*, London: Routledge.

O'Neill, M and Conlon, M (2016) *Walking with Michael Conlon in Belfast*. https://walkingborders.com/walk-5-walking-in-belfast-with-michael-conlon/

O'Neill, M, Giddens, S, Breatnach, P, Bagley, C, Bourne, M, and Judge, T (2001) 'Renewed Methodologies for Social Research: Ethno-mimesis as Performative Praxis', *Sociological Review* 50(1): 75–88.

O'Neill, M and Hill, I (nd) http://ghostsofourfuture.com/.

O'Neill, M and Hubbard, P (2010) 'Walking, Sensing, Belonging: Ethno-mimesis as Performative Praxis', *Visual Studies*, 25(1): 46–58.

O'Neill, M and Laing, M (2018) 'Sex Worker Rights, Recognition and Resistance: Towards a "Real Politics of Justice"' in S Fitzgerald and K McGarry (eds) *Realising Justice for Sex Workers*, London: Rowman and Littlefield.

O'Neill, M and Perivolaris, J (2016) Walking with Photographer John Perivolaris in Chios: www.walkingborders.com.

O'Neill, M and Porth, K (2016) Walk 7. Walking with Kerry Porth at the Missing Women's Memorial Walk in Vancouver. https://www.walkingborders.com/?p=397 (accessed 15 February 2019).

O'Neill, M and Roberts, B (2019) *Walking Methods: Research on the Move*, London: Routledge.

O'Neill, M, Roberts, B and Sparkes, A (2015) *Advances in Biographical Methods – Creative Applications*, London: Palgrave.

O'Neill, M and Seal, L (2012) *Transgressive Imaginations: Crime, Deviance and Culture*, Basingstoke: Palgrave.

O'Neill, M and Stenning, P (2014) 'Walking Biographies and Innovations in visual and Participatory Methods: Community, Politics and Resistance in Downtown East Side Vancouver', in C Heinz and Ghornung (eds) *The Medialization of Auto/Biographies:Different Forms and their Communicative Contexts*, Hamburg: UVK.

O'Sullivan, E and O'Donnell, I (2007) 'Coercive Confinement in the Republic of Ireland: The Waning of a Culture of Control', *Punishment & Society*, 9(1): 27–48.

O'Sullivan, E and O'Donnell, I (2012) *Coercive Confinement in Ireland: Patients, prisoners and penitents*, Manchester: Manchester University Press.

O'Toole, F (2003) 'Sisters of No Mercy', *The Observer*, 16 February: https://www.theguardian.com/film/2003/feb/16/features.review1.

Orwell, G (1949) *1984*, London: Secker and Warburg.

Page, J and Goodman, P (2018) 'Creative Disruption: Edward Bunker, Carceral Habitus, and the Criminological Value of Fiction', *Theoretical Criminology*, doi/pdf/10.1177/1362480618769866.

Pharr, MF and Clark, LA (2012) 'Introduction', in MF Pharr and LA Clark (eds) *Of Bread, Blood and the Hunger Games*, Jefferson, NC: McFarland, pp 5–19.

Philomena (2013) Dir Stephen Frears [Film] UK: 20th Century Fox.

Piamonte, S (2015) 'The Criminological Imagination and the Promise of Fiction', in J Frauley (ed) *C Wright Mills and the Criminological Imagination: Prospects for Creative Inquiry*, Farnham: Ashgate, pp 241–54.

Pickering, S (2005) *Refugees and State Crime*. Annandale, NSW, Australia: The Federation Press.

Pilkington Garimara, D (2002 [2013]) *Follow the Rabbit Proof Fence*, St Lucia: University of Queensland Press.

Pine, E (2011) *The Politics of Irish Memory: Performing Remembrance in Contemporary Irish Culture*, London: Palgrave.

Pink, S (2007) 'Walking with Video', *Visual Studies*, 22(3): 240–52.

Pink, S, Hubbard, P, O'Neill, M and Radley, A (2010) 'Walking Across Disciplines: From Ethnography to Arts Practice', *Visual Studies*, 25(1): 1–7.

Porth, K and O'Neill, M (2016) *Walking with Kerry Porth at the Missing Women's Memorial March in Vancouver.* https://walkingborders. com/walk-7walking-with-kerry-porth-at-the-missing-womens-memorial-walk-in-vancouver/.

Presser, L, Sandberg, S (eds) (2015) *Narrative Criminology: Understanding Stories of Crime*, New York: New York University Press.

Pulliam, J (2014) 'Real or Not Real – Katniss Everdeen Loves Peeta Mellark: The Lingering Effects of Discipline in the Hunger Games Trilogy' in SK Day, MA Green-Barteet and AL Montz (eds) *Female Rebellion in Young Adult Fiction*, London: Routledge, pp 171–85.

Qualmann, C and O'Neill, M (2017) Walk 11. Walking with Clare Qualmann, https://www.walkingborders.com/?p=559 (accessed 15 February 2019).

Rabbit Proof Fence (2002) Dir Philip Noyce [Film] Australia: Becker Entertainment.

Rafter, N (2006) *Shots in the Mirror: Crime Films and Society*, Oxford: Oxford University Press. 2nd edition.

Rafter, N (2007) 'Crime, Film and Criminology: Recent Sex-crime Movies', *Theoretical Criminology*, 11(3): 403–20.

Rafter, N and Brown, M (2011) *Criminology Goes to the Movies*, New York: New York University Press.

Ritzer, G (1998) 'Writing to Be Read: Changing the Culture and Reward of American Sociology', *Contemporary Sociology*, 27(5): 446–53.

Roberts, B (2015) 'Biographical Research: Past, Present, Future' in M O'Neill, B Roberts and A Sparkes (eds) *Advances in Biographical Methods – Creative Applications*, London: Palgrave.

Rosa, H (2013) *Social Acceleration*, New York: Columbia University Press.

Rose, G (1996) 'As If the Mirrors had Bled: Masculine Dwelling, Masculinist Theory and Feminist Masquerade', in N Duncan (ed) *Body Space: Destabilising Geographies of Gender and Sexuality*, London: Routledge, pp 57–74.

Roszak, S (2016) 'Coming of Age in a Divided City: Cultural Hybridity and Ethnic Injustice in Sandra Cisneros and Veronica Roth', *Children's Literature*, 44: 61–77.

Roth, V (2011) *Divergent*, New York: Katherine Tegen Books.

Rothman, J (2016) 'The Lives of Poor White People', *The New Yorker*, 12 September: https://www.newyorker.com/culture/cultural-comment/the-lives-of-poor-white-people.

Rowe, DL (2004) 'From Inside Out: Women Writers Behind Prison Walls', unpublished PhD thesis, University of Maryland.

Royal Canadian Mounted Police (2014) *Missing and Murdered Aboriginal Women: A National Operational Overview.* http://www.rcmp-grc.gc.ca/en/missing-and-murdered-aboriginal-women-national-operational-overview.

Rucka, G, Lark, M and Arcas, S (2013-ongoing) *Lazarus*, Portland, OR: Image Comics.

Ruggiero, V (2003) *Crime in Literature: Sociology of Deviance and Fiction*, London: Verso.

Ruggiero, V (2012) 'Victor Hugo and Octave Mirbeau: A Sociological Analysis of Imprisonment Fiction', in L Cheliotis (ed) *The Arts of Imprisonment: Control, Resistance and Empowerment*, London: Routledge, pp 246–61.

Ruggiero, V (2015) 'Balzac and the Crimes of the Powerful', *Societies*, 5(2): 325–38.

Ruggiero, V (2018) 'Fiction, War and Criminology', *Criminology and Criminal Justice,* doi/pdf/10.1177/1748895818781198.

Sales, R. (2007) *Understanding Immigration and Refugee Policy: Contradicitions and Continuities*, Bristol: Policy Press.

Scarleta, J (2014) *Rethinking Occupied Ireland: Gender and Incarceration in Contemporary Irish Film*, Syracuse, NY: Syracuse University Press.

Schindler's List (1993) Dir Steven Spielberg [Film] USA: Universal Pictures.

Scott, RR (2009) 'Appalachia and the Construction of Whiteness in the United States', *Sociology Compass*, 3(5): 803–10.

Scott, S (2010) 'Revisiting the Total Institution: Performative Regulation in the Reinventive Institution', *Sociology*, 44(2): 213–31.

Scott, S (2011) *Total Institutions and Reinvented Identities*, Basingstoke: Palgrave.

Seal, L (2010) *Women, Murder and Femininity: Gender Representations of Women Who Kill*, Basingstoke: Palgrave.

Seal, L (2014) *Capital Punishment in Twentieth Century Britain: Audience, Justice, Memory*, London: Routledge.

Senior, J (2016) 'In "Hillbilly Elegy", A Tough Love Analysis of the Poor Who Back Trump', *New York Times*, 10 August: https://www.nytimes.com/2016/08/11/books/review-in-hillbilly-elegy-a-compassionate-analysis-of-the-poor-who-love-trump.html?_r=0.

Shields, R (1991) *Places on the Margin: Alternative Geographies of Modernity*, London: Routledge.

Simmons, AM (2012) 'Class on Fire: Using the Hunger Games Trilogy to Encourage Social Action', *Journal of Adolescent and Adult Literacy*, 56(1): 22–34.

Simms, H (2001) Herb Simms interviewed by John Maynard for the Bringing them home oral history project [sound recording], Oral TRC 950973: http://nla.gov.au/nla.obj-218419195/listen.

Simpson, AV, Clegg, SR, Lopes, MP, De Cunha, M, Rego, A and Pitsis, T (2014) 'Doing Compassion or Doing Discipline? Power Relations and the Magdalene Laundries', *Journal of Political Power*, 7(2): 253–74.

Sixsmith, M (2009) *The Lost Child of Philomena Lee*, London: Macmillan.

Smith, AM (1998) *Laclau and Mouffe: The Radical Democratic Imaginary*, London: Routledge.

Smith, D (2006) *Globalization: The Hidden Agenda*, Cambridge: Polity.

Smith, JM (2007) *Ireland's Magdalen Laundries*, Manchester: Manchester University Press.

Soto, C (2017) 'Poetry in the Age of Mass Incarceration: Challenging the Dichotomy of Innocence Versus Criminality', *Poetry Foundation*: https://www.poetryfoundation.org/harriet/2017/09/poetry-in-the-age-of-mass-incarceration-challenging-the-dichotomy-of-innocence-versus-criminality.

Stallybrass, P and White, A (1986) *The Politics and Poetics of Transgression*, London: Methuen.

Stevens, E (2000) Eileen Stevens interviewed by Steven Guth for the Bringing them home oral history project [sound recording], Oral TRC 1895972: http://nla.gov.au/nla.obj-218279027/listen.

Stone, D (2017) *Concentration Camps: A Short History*, Oxford: Oxford University Press.

Strauss, C (2006) 'The Imaginary', *Anthropological Theory*, 6(3): 322–44.

Taber, N, Woloshyn, V and Lane, L (2013) '"She's more like a guy" and "he's more like a teddy bear": Girls' Perception of Violence and Gender in The Hunger Games', *Journal of Youth Studies*, 16(8): 1022–37.

Takami, K (1999) *Battle Royale*, Tokyo: Ohta Publishing.

Tan, SSM (2013) 'Burn with Us: Sacrificing Childhood in The Hunger Games', *The Lion and the Unicorn*, 37(1): 54–73.

Tassioglou, E and Dobrowlesky, A (2006) *Women, Migration and Citizenship*, London: Routledge.

The Handmaid's Tale (2017; 2018) Hulu.

The Magdalene Sisters (2002) Dir Peter Mullan [Film] USA: Miramax.

The Running Man (1987) Dir Paul Glaser [Film] USA: TriStar Pictures.

The Women's Memorial March (2016) *February 14th Memorial March* https://womensmemorialmarch.wordpress.com/.

Thomson, A (2007) 'Four Paradigm Transformations in Oral History', *The Oral History Review*, 34(1): 49–70.

Till, KE and Kearns, G (2016) 'Emplacing "who we are, what we are": The Embodied and Historical Geographies of ANU Productions', *Laundry, Landscape Values: Place and Praxis*, NUI Galway: Centre for Landscape Studies, pp 363–8.

Travis, A (2014) 'Prison Book Ban Is Unlawful, Court Rules', *The Guardian*, 5 December: https://www.theguardian.com/society/2014/dec/05/prison-book-ban-unlawful-court-chris-grayling.

Tucker, Jr, KH (2005) 'From the Imaginary to Subjectification: Castoriadis and Touraine on the Performative Public Sphere', *Thesis Eleven*, 8(3): 42–60.

Turner, V (1967) 'Betwixt and Between: The Liminal Period in Rites de Passage', in *The Forest of Symbols*. Ithaca, NY: Cornell University Press.

Tyler, I (2013) *Revolting Subjects: Social Abjection and Resistance in Neoliberal Britain*, London: Zed Books.

Tyler, I (2018) 'The Hieroglyphics of the Border: Racial Stigma in Neoliberal Europe', *Ethnic and Racial Studies*, 41(10): 1783–801.

UNHCR (2018) *Desperate Journeys: Refugees and migrants arriving in Europe and at Europe's Borders*, UNHCR.

Urry, J (2007) *Mobilities*, Cambridge: Polity.

van Gennep, A (1960) *The Rites of Passage*. Chicago, IL: University of Chicago Press.

van Krieken, R (1999a) 'The "Stolen Generations" and Cultural Genocide', *Childhood*, 6(3): 297–311.

van Krieken, R (1999b) 'The Barbarism of civilization: Cultural Genocide and the "Stolen Generations"', *British Journal of Sociology*, 50(2): 297–315.

Vance, JD (2016) *Hillbilly Elegy*, New York: Harper.

Vostal, F (2016) *Accelerating Academia: The Changing Structure of Academic Time*, London: Palgrave.

Wahidin, A and Tate, S (2005) 'Prison (E)scapes and Body Tropes: Older Women and the Prison Time Machine', *Body and Society*, 11(2): 59–79.

Walklate, S and Jacobsen, M (2017) 'Introduction: Introducing Liquid Criminology', in MH Jacobsen and S Walklate (eds) *Liquid Criminology: Doing Imaginative Criminological Research*, London: Routledge, pp 1–13.

Walklate, S, McGarry, R and Mythen, G (2016) 'Trauma, Visual Criminology and the Poetics of Justice', in MH Jacobsen (ed) *The Poetics of Crime: Understanding and Researching Deviance*, Farnham: Ashgate, pp 263–83.

Walkowitz, J (1980) *Prostitution and Victorian Society*, Cambridge: Cambridge University Press.

Walters, R (2003) *Deviant Knowledge: Criminology, Politics and Policy*, Cullompton: Willan.

Wang, J (2018) *Carceral Capitalism*, Cambridge, MA: MIT Press.

Warf, B and Arias, S (2009) 'Introduction: The Reinsertion of Space into the Social Sciences and Humanities', in B Warf and S Arias (eds) *The Spatial Turn: Interdisciplinary Perspectives*, London: Routledge, pp 1–10.

Weigel, S (1996) *Body and Image-Space: Re-reading Walter Benjamin*, London: Routledge.

Wezner, K (2012) '"Perhaps I am Watching You Now": Panem's Panopticons', in MF Pharr and LA Clark (eds) *Of Bread, Blood and the Hunger Games*, Jefferson, NC: McFarland, pp 148–57.

Whitbourn, M (2016) 'Baird Government to Offer Reparations to Stolen Generations', *The Sydney Morning Herald*, 2 December: http://www.smh.com.au/nsw/baird-government-to-offer-reparations-to-stolen-generations-20161201-gt1luq.html.

Wilmer, SE (2016) 'Biopolitics at the Laundry: Ireland's Unwed Mothers', in SE Wilmer and A Zukauskiate (eds) *Resisting Biopolitics: Philosophical, Political, and Performative Strategies*, London: Routledge, pp 254–70.

Winnicott, ID (1951) *Playing and Reality*, London: Routledge.

Winter, S (2017) 'Two Models of Monetary Redress: A Structural Analysis', Victims and Offenders: http://dx.doi.org/10.1080/1556 4886.2017.1280108.

Witness: Sex in a Cold Climate (1998) Channel 4.

Woodrow, M (1999) Marjorie Woodrow interviewed by Colleen Hattersley for the Bringing them home oral history project [sound recording] Oral TRC 296804: http://nla.gov.au/nla.obj-218208552/ listen.

Wright, R (1940) *Native Son*, New York: Harper.

Wright Mills, C (1959 [1970]) *The Sociological Imagination*, Oxford: Oxford University Press.

Yeager, J and Culleton, J (2016) 'Gendered Violence and Cultural Forgetting: The Case of the Irish Magdalenes', *Radical History Review*, 126: 134–46.

Young, A (1996) *Imagining Crime: Textural Outlaws and Criminal Conversations*, London: Sage.

Young, A (2004) *Judging the Image: Art, Value, and Law*, London: Routledge.

Young, A (2008) 'Culture, Critical Criminology and the Imagination of Crime', in T Anthony and C Cuneen (eds) *The Critical Criminology Companion*, Sydney: Hawkins Press.

Young, J (2011) *The Criminological Imagination*, Cambridge: Polity.

Young, R (1994) *Mental Space*, Process Press.

Yuval-Davis, N and Stoetzler, M (2002) 'Imagined Boundaries and Borders: A Gendered Gaze', *European Journal of Women's Studies*, 9(3): 329–44.

Index